# GOOD PASTOR, BAD FIT

MAINTAINING PASTORAL AUTHENTICITY
THROUGH RESIGNATION AND
TERMINATION

## MICHAEL W. PALMER

FOREWORD BY REV. DR. WILLIAM L. LEE

WESTBOW
PRESS®
A DIVISION OF THOMAS NELSON
& ZONDERVAN

WestBow Press books may be ordered through booksellers or by contacting:

WestBow Press
A Division of Thomas Nelson & Zondervan
1663 Liberty Drive
Bloomington, IN 47403
www.westbowpress.com
844-714-3454

ISBN: 978-1-9736-9902-6 (sc)
ISBN: 978-1-9736-9901-9 (hc)
ISBN: 978-1-9736-9903-3 (e)

Library of Congress Control Number: 2023909648

Print information available on the last page.

WestBow Press rev. date: 08/08/2023

*To my wife, Lisa and our son, Michael Jr.*

*To my parents, Roy, Jr. and Dorothy Jane Palmer*

*In memory of Mrs. Darnelle Gates, Pastor Joseph A. Keaton, and Pastor Herman L. Word Sr.*

*Thanks to the pastors who willingly stepped into this "empty space."*

# CONTENTS

# FOREWORD

I have a simple rule of thumb for justifying the purchase of a book. If the book affords me at least one idea or concept that causes me to think differently or dig deeper, then it is worth the cost. Occasionally, I encounter a book where on each page I highlight at least one line that stirs my imagination and causes my cognitive juices to churn. *Good Pastor, Bad Fit* is such a book.

In reading *Good Pastor, Bad Fit*, the word "authentic" becomes a travel companion throughout the book. Michael Palmer's focus is maintaining pastoral authenticity through resignation and termination. I contend that this book helps us to deal with our own authenticity long before resignation and termination become options. Honestly, if the preacher/pastor/minister does not seek to discover who they are early in their careers, they won't have an authentic self to anchor during turbulent moments in ministry.

The way the author introduces Job as the biblical foundation for this book is pure genius. I have been in ministry for over fifty years and the novel way that Michael narrates the Job story is refreshing for those who seek to maintain pastoral authenticity through resignation and termination. Job is not a pastor, Michael writes, but is a model of integrity and authenticity during difficult times. *Good Pastor,*

*Bad Fit* becomes prescription lenses for us to do a reread of Job. My personal conviction is that all who read this book will be able to say like Job, "But he knows the way that I take; when he has tested me, I will come forth as gold." (Job 23:10 NIV)

Michael Palmer knows the way that pastors take, especially when we must discern when it is time for resignation or termination. He allows us to stand on the balcony and view his struggle, pain, and hurt. From the balcony of *Good Pastor, Bad Fit*, we see more than the negative aspect of Michael's journey. We see how during and after the test, he came forth as gold. In truth, he has taught us that a resignation does not mean we have resigned ministry and that termination is not terminal. A good fit awaits a good pastor who maintains their authenticity through resignation and termination.

*Good Pastor, Bad Fit* is a good fit for those discerning a call, contemplating your first pastoral assignment, search committees, and especially those who know they are compromising their authentic selves in a toxic ministry. I encourage you to try *Good Pastor, Bad Fit* on for size and discover how uncomfortably comfortable this book is.

Rev. Dr. William L. Lee

*Retired Pastor, Loudon Avenue Christian Church, Roanoke, Virginia Director, Certificate in African American Ministry, Lexington Theological Seminary, Lexington, Kentucky*

# PREFACE

I began working on this project after resigning from a church that I could no longer pastor without compromising my personal values. Although this was an extremely difficult decision, I was confident it was the right one when I heard very clearly from God that I could not remain there and continue to be who He created and called me to be. This also assisted me in shifting my focus from justifiably blaming certain leaders and congregants to trusting God in doing what was best for me in maintaining my authenticity during my transition.

In researching the ability of pastors to maintain their pastoral authenticity through resignation and termination, interviews were conducted with pastors to discuss relative individual experiences and explore best practices for dealing with church conflict and congregational hostility leading to resignation and termination. The research revealed, among other things, the need to create space for discussion, confession, and exploration for pastors facing the hardships associated with forced resignation and termination. The participating pastors also offered advice for pastors who may encounter similar situations.

Biblical/theological relevance was explored in researching the authenticity of Job. Though he was not a pastoral figure, Job's ability to maintain his spiritual and relational authenticity through significant lifestyle changes provides examples for pastors facing the life-changing transitions this project addresses.

# INTRODUCTION

God has given pastors gifts consistent with their calling to lead specific congregations. But stories are often told of pastors who experience congregational conflict and hostility that lead to the suppression of their pastoral gifts and personalities. The subsequent outcome is a decline in, or complete absence of, pastoral authenticity that often results in pastors transitioning from churches either by resignation or termination. Using my personal pastoral resignation in the face of internal conflict and hostility, and similar experiences of other pastors, this project addresses maintaining pastoral authenticity through resignation and termination as a means to spiritual growth.

While navigating my personal experience related to this project (outlined in chapter 1), I discovered that there are numerous resources addressing the difficulties associated with pastoring. Most of them are written to help pastors work through and hopefully overcome the challenges often associated with pastoring with the intent of continuing in their current employ. However, I was only able to locate a limited number of helpful resources that addressed the specific act of transitioning from a church by choice or by force, which led me to create a resource through the completion of this project.

Chapter 1 names and unfolds the condition of my project by providing detailed information about my past vocational experiences that contributed to the development of my authentic self and the pastoral experiences that led to my resignation from a church in the face of internal hostility. While my intent is not to use this chapter as an opportunity to engage in church bashing, it is necessary to provide accurate details that highlight the existence of unnamed members and leaders who were intentionally hostile. This chapter also defines authenticity and outlines what it means to "practice" authenticity both from a general perspective and one that is more pastor-specific.

Chapter 2 is the biblical/theological chapter in which I show biblical relevance to this project by focusing on the authenticity of Job. While Job did not assume a pastoral role, his ability to maintain his spiritual and relational authenticity through significant life changes speaks directly to this project and provides additional opportunities to focus on authenticity from a broader perspective rather than solely from a pastor-specific point of view. Job is introduced as a man who was blameless, upright, feared God, and shunned evil, which speaks of his integrity, his treatment of others, his religion, and his morality. This chapter focuses primarily on these four areas describing Job's constant nature and provides relevant examples and helpful information for pastors who are facing difficult life-changing transitions.

My main theological concern is Job's ability to maintain his authenticity in extremely difficult times by consistently exercising the already existing character traits he displayed prior to Satan's interference. The conclusion of this chapter acknowledges that in what appears to have been the most spiritually, physically, emotionally challenging, and excruciatingly painful time of his life, Job does not become a new or different Job. Instead, he continues living as the authentic man God created him to be through the daily practice of authenticity.

It is imperative that pastors understand not only *what we are* vocationally, but also *who we are* related to our calling, especially when forced to consider transitioning from a church. Our calling as pastors is not a simple matter of God "matching" us with specific congregations. It is about His carefully placing us within a body of believers where our God-given gifts can best be used to make disciples and glorify God. Providing this understanding may also proactively assist pastors in accepting positions that are the best fit for their authentic selves.

Chapter 3 includes information attained from interviewing several pastors with past or current experiences related to the condition this project addresses. While most of the pastors who were interviewed had already left the churches in question and continued in the pastoral ministry, one interview was conducted with a pastor who had successfully pursued a career in another field and, at the time of the interview, was extremely pleased with his decision to follow God in doing so. As part of the interview process, a signed consent form was obtained from each of the interviewees containing the following information:

> **Title:** Maintaining Pastoral Authenticity through Resignation and Termination
>
> **Purpose:** To explore various transitional experiences ultimately resulting in the development and implementation of workshops, courses, and/

or other publications that will assist pastors in understanding and maintaining their authenticity through resignation and termination.

**Procedure & Time Requirement:** If you consent, you will be asked several questions in an oral interview at a date, time, and location that is convenient for you. I may make an audio recording of the interview that will only be used for accurate written documentation. The interview will take approximately 1–2 hours of your time, including any necessary follow-up conversations by phone, text, or email.

**Voluntary Participation:** Your participation in this project is completely voluntary. If you choose to participate, you may still decline to answer any of the interview questions that you do not want to answer. You may also withdraw from this project at any time.

**Confidentiality/Anonymity:** Your name will be kept confidential in all the reporting and documentation related to this study. I will be the only person present for the interview and the only person who listens to any audio recordings. I will use pseudonyms—fictitious names—for all participants.

**Risks:** There are no known risks associated with this interview.

**Benefits:** While there are no guaranteed benefits, it is possible that you will experience a sense of purpose and relief in knowing that sharing your answers to the interview questions may eventually benefit pastors with similar experiences.

**Sharing the Results:** I plan to construct a written account of what I learn from my interviews, reading, research, and other collected data. This information (using pseudonyms) will be submitted to my WTS Faculty Reader and the Doctor of Ministry Committee at scheduled times during this process.

**Publication:** The final version of this project will be submitted to the WTS Library and posted publicly in the Theological Research Exchange Network (TREN), where all WTS Doctor of Ministry projects have been preserved since 2011. There is also the possibility that I will publish this project or refer to it in published writings in the future. If so, I will continue to use pseudonyms and may alter some personal and professional identifying details to further protect your anonymity.

**Consent:** By signing below, you are agreeing to an interview for this project. Be sure that any questions you may have related to my project are answered to your satisfaction prior to signing. If you agree to participate in this project, a copy of this consent document will be given to you.

Although each of the interviewees was given the option of withdrawing from this project at any time, all of them participated without interruption. Any surprising or unexpected findings or developments relative to this project are also included in this chapter.

Chapter 4 addresses the healing associated with "the creation of an empty space" and is comprised of conclusions reached from the research and interviews mentioned in chapter 3. This chapter also includes recommendations for anyone who is considering conducting a similar project. Items that were part of this project such as the interview consent form and the interview questions are included as appendices.

The ultimate goal of this project is to encourage pastors to remain true to who God not only *called* them to be, but also to be true to who God *created* them to be. Acknowledging how easy it is to become entangled in the status and celebrity of the pastorate, this project hopefully serves as a reminder to remain grounded in the fundamental values with which most of us accepted the call of God to lead others to lifelong faith in Jesus Christ.

# CHAPTER 1

# PRACTICING AUTHENTICITY

According to the author and motivational speaker Mike Robbins,

> Authenticity is a process. It's something that continues to evolve throughout our entire lives. We can't become "authentic" in the same way we can earn a degree or accomplish a financial goal. Authenticity—like love, health, courage, awareness, patience, and more—is an ideal we aspire to and is something we must practice in the moment-by-moment, day-by-day experiences of life. Our ability to be real can and will deepen as we move through our journey of life, if we're conscious about it. Becoming more of who we really are is a process that never ends.[1]

---

[1] Mike Robbins, *Be Yourself, Everyone Else Is Already Taken: Transform Your Life with the Power of Authenticity* (San Francisco: Jossey-Bass, 2009), 4.

This idea of authenticity being a process, coupled with the need to practice it daily, may be a hard pill to swallow for those who have come to understand authenticity as a defining characteristic that once attained is a constant one that needs to be openly and regularly displayed before others and not necessarily practiced. Contrary to Robbins's statement above, many people believe becoming authentic is done *very much* like earning a degree or accomplishing a financial goal. This was certainly true for me as I entered adulthood and began serving in the US Army. My understanding of being authentic up to that point in my life was simply about remaining true to who I had known myself to be. Little did I know, I had also entered the never-ending process and practice of authenticity that would prove beneficial in my development as a leader in *the military, law enforcement*, and *the pastorate*. Having practiced authenticity for years would also prove beneficial during the most difficult experience of my pastoral career, which led to my resignation from a church and is the focus of this project.

## ■ THE MILITARY

One of the goals of basic training in the US Army during my enlistment was to strip a person of who they are upon arrival and send them away with a new perspective, produced and guided by military principles—such as discipline, courage, honor, and teamwork. Eating, sleeping, cleaning, marching, and training were all accomplished as a team, and nothing short of excellence was acceptable. If one of us succeeded, we all succeeded, resulting in a reward for all. In turn, if one of us failed, we all failed, resulting in discipline for all. For me, nothing was more effective in promoting teamwork than being disciplined for the faults or failures of others.

One such incident occurred when a member of my platoon was caught hiding fireworks in a trash can in our barracks. Where and why he had purchased fireworks was a mystery since our training ran from January through May—nowhere near Independence Day or any other holidays that would justify stockpiling fireworks. Nonetheless, we were all disciplined for his foolishness by having to move every existing item—bunks, lockers, cabinets, uniforms, personal clothing, tables, desks, etc.—by stairs from our third-floor bay to the lower-level exterior platform. Once the bay was completely emptied, our assignment was to strip and wax the floor and return everything to its original location without leaving so much as a scratch on the newly polished floor. As you can imagine, this form of collective discipline caused tempers to flare and fights to ensue, prolonging both the pain and the process.

Amid the chaos, however, were some positive outcomes. One was the noticeable leadership potential demonstrated by some of us during this hectic experience. Likely by design, this disciplinary procedure afforded our drill instructors the opportunity to distinguish between the leaders and followers in our platoon. I was singled out as one of the leaders. With that, things immediately began to change as I was not only placed in positions of authority within our platoon but I was also exposed to the reality that more was expected of me and that I could no longer act like everyone else. For the first time, I was being held responsible for the well-being of others who were not my two younger brothers while also being held accountable for their successes and failures. Unknown to me at the time, this is when I began my journey of practicing authenticity.

I often share with others stories of my experiences while serving as a soldier. Something I always express is how appreciative I am for the mental and emotional growth I experienced during my years of service. Numerous events and encounters—both positive and negative—contributed to my becoming increasingly mature and responsible. Being young, I of course made occasional immature decisions and behaved irresponsibly. However, I learned with each mistake how to take responsibility for my actions and make the necessary corrections to avoid repeating those mistakes. With each event, encounter, and experience, I learned increasingly more about myself—the good, the bad, and the ugly. During this formative period, I worked hard to develop an authentic identity and found that becoming an effective and influential leader requires an especially important character trait: *integrity.*

As I matured and learned more about what it meant to have integrity, I discovered the importance and necessity of continually looking inwardly with the purpose of acknowledging and evaluating my own character deficiencies instead of looking outside myself to explain or even justify them. In summarizing his "Five Principles of Authenticity"—know yourself, transform your fear, express yourself, be bold, and celebrate who you are—Robbins says,

> Knowing ourselves is the first step to being ourselves in an authentic way. It takes courage to really look within and become aware of who we truly are at the deepest level. Our commitment to personal growth, to discover more of who we really are, and to allow the support, honest feedback, and guidance

of others is essential in our ability to know ourselves
and thus be authentic.[2]

Having been honorably discharged with plenty of room for growth and maturity, the army is where I began moving from simply knowing *about* myself to embarking on my journey of self-awareness.

## ■ LAW ENFORCEMENT

My level of self-awareness was heightened significantly during my service in law enforcement immediately following my time in the military. Although most of my experiences and interactions were positive, it was through the occasional negative experiences that I began to confidently and unashamedly appreciate my identity, particularly as an African American man.

One of the things that always bothered me during my service as a police officer was the idea that we were all "blue." When it came to the subject of race, I would often hear some of my colleagues say they did not see color because we were all blue, referring to the traditional color of the police uniform and the brotherhood it continues to symbolize. While I appreciated the spirit of brotherhood in which this statement was made, I often responded by explaining my belief that ignoring or dismissing the color of one's skin limited our ability to really know the person *in* the uniform.

My employment was part of this predominately white department's efforts to increase racial diversity in its workforce by recruiting minorities. As expected, cultural differences created occasional rifts that presented opportunities for learning and growth

---

[2] Robbins, *Be Yourself, Everyone Else Is Already Taken*, 226.

for individuals and the department. These personal experiences—both positive and negative—impacted how I viewed others and how I viewed and valued myself. I eventually learned the particularly important lesson that my authenticity was tied not only to the self-awareness I gained during my army enlistment but also to my self-acceptance. Accepting myself in that environment was about making peace with *all* of who I was in spite of the beliefs and behaviors of others. It also afforded me a sense of freedom from any anxieties and a deeper awareness and appreciation of myself.

Although practicing authenticity with increasing self-awareness and self-acceptance was enriching, it also came with a certain degree of risk. Some of my relationships suffered as friends and coworkers struggled to make sense of the changes I was making. Little did they know, I also struggled to make sense of some of my own behavioral and conversational changes involved with practicing authenticity. These internal struggles were often accompanied by feelings of self-doubt and questioning whether the changes and struggles were worth the effort. Fortunately, while all this was occurring, I was invited to church by a friend and eventually gave my life to Jesus Christ. The spiritual guidance, clarity, and confirmation I experienced were exactly what I needed to further my journey of practicing authenticity. Brené Brown wrote in *The Gifts of Imperfection*, "Mindfully practicing authenticity during our most soul-searching struggles is how we invite grace, joy, and gratitude into our lives."[3] With grace, joy, and gratitude becoming more of a factor in my decision-making, I later accepted God's call to ministry

---

[3] Brené Brown, *The Gifts of Imperfection: Let Go of Who You Think You're Supposed to Be and Embrace Who You Are* (Center City, MN: Hazelden Publishing 2010), 50.

and subsequently entered the pastorate, where I naively assumed authenticity was welcomed and appreciated by all.

## ■ THE PASTORATE

In an online article entitled "10 Real Reasons Pastors Quit Too Soon," Tim Peters opens by stating, "More than 1,700 pastors leave the ministry every month."[4] Others have argued that the more realistic number is closer to 250 per month. Either way, the number of pastors who are leaving churches within five years is concerning. The lists of reasons given by various writers may differ slightly but are relatively consistent across the board. Peters's list includes the following:

1. Discouragement. When you hear criticism and look out to see empty pews, it can be difficult to recognize the positive impact you're making.
2. Failure. Many pastors have difficulty recognizing success. They compare themselves to other pastors and other ministries. The key is not to compare but to celebrate your successes.
3. Loneliness. With so many people looking to pastors for guidance, it can be difficult for pastors to let their guard down. They don't want to come across as less than perfect.

---

[4] Tim Peters, "10 Reasons Why Pastors Quit Too Soon," *Church Leaders* (April 2016), accessed September 16, 2019, https://churchleaders.com/pastors/pastor-articles/161343-tim_peters_10_common_reasons_pastors_quit_too_soon.html.

They feel they can't be transparent and vulnerable. That creates a sense of isolation.

4. Moral Failure. The moral failures of pastors are magnified more than the average person. The key to avoiding moral failures is creating a system of risk prevention.

5. Financial Pressure. Most ministries are nonprofits, so pastors are not compensated well. When you can't fully provide the life you want for your family, it makes it hard to continue.

6. Anger. When things aren't going well, pastors become angry—with others, themselves, or God. The worst thing about anger is it spreads like wildfire. The medicine for anger is forgiveness. We have to forgive so we can move on.

7. Burnout. Pastors are put on a treadmill. They go from the ministry to a hospital visit to writing a sermon to meeting with congregation members. They just keep running until there's no passion or energy left. They can become exhausted and depleted.

8. Physical Health. Many pastors overwork themselves and simply do not care for their bodies. When you're busy, it's easy to eat poorly. But eating the right foods is essential to physical health. It's the difference between fueling the body and depleting the body. Pastors don't get enough rest or regular exercise. Exercise makes a huge difference in physical and mental health.

9. Marriage/Family Problems. Too often, a pastor's spouse and children end up taking a backseat to the ministry. The key is balance. Marriage has to be a top priority. Your relationship with your spouse is the most important relationship you have on this earth. You have to nurture your family

relationships—whether that means having family night or seeking counseling.

10. Too Busy/Driven. A lot of pastors simply are not working efficiently. They are not protecting their calendars or giving themselves the space they need. They haven't learned how to say "no." Being busy is not always being productive. Pastors need to find ways to maximize their time.[5]

Nearing the close of my thirteenth year as a pastor, and experiencing difficulties in two of the areas mentioned above, I prayerfully began exploring other pastoral employment opportunities. Completely confident that I was being obedient to God's calling, I landed at a church where I later found myself wrestling again with deciding between staying or leaving. On this occasion, my decision was based on a reason I have yet to find on any list similar to the one above. I eventually resigned because the only way for me to continue serving at this church was for me to compromise my pastoral authenticity—to become someone God did not create or call me to be.

In revealing the circumstances that led to my departure from this particular church, it is imperative that I express my sincere appreciation for the many church and community members with whom I enjoyed spiritually and emotionally enriching relationships. There were several members of the church who supported me until the very end of my employment and beyond—some of whom assisted me in gathering my belongings from my office on my final

---

[5] Peters, *Why Pastors Quit*, https://churchleaders.com/pastors/pastor-articles/161343-tim_peters_10_common_reasons_pastors_quit_too_soon.html.

day. Years later, I still maintain relationships with some of them who also terminated their church memberships and are actively serving God as members of other local congregations. Others remained loyal to this church with the hope of influencing positive change.

While enduring the often slow and disconcerting nature of the traditional pastoral search process followed by many churches, there were red flags indicating the church's extreme focus on the past that I initially viewed as a manageable obstacle. Though these warnings and some of the church leaders involved would eventually impact my decision to resign years later, I have no doubts about God's desire for me to serve as the pastor of this church, even though it was for a relatively brief period of time. As challenging as it occasionally was, my time there was full of lessons to be learned specifically through the testing of my authenticity. As stated before, it also afforded me opportunities for new and lasting personal and professional relationships.

During the application process and my initial months on the job, I learned that the church in question was an extremely traditional church that seemed to be driven more by religious practices and self-imposed traditions than biblical principles. There was a general belief that things had to occur according to an internally created playbook—officially identified as the constitution and by-laws—that seemed to be written, repeatedly revised, and interpreted to maintain certain practices and empower certain people. Even after learning about their peculiar culture and having over a decade of pastoral experience, I was still confident (and maybe a bit naïve) in believing I could lead this church to a stronger faith and obedience to God's word in making disciples, especially within the immediate community.

Like many others, this church had a rich history that began with a few faithful Christians exercising their obedience to God's calling for them to establish a local congregation. Committed to prayer, the Word of God, and the leading of the Holy Spirit, these believers steadfastly evangelized and discipled others as, over the years, their church evolved into a meaningful community partner. Over time, however, people moved away from this once close-knit community, contributing to demographic changes and cultural preferences that differed significantly from the church's traditional beliefs and practices. Some had not only left the community, but they also ignored the changes, needs, and pressing concerns throughout the neighborhood as they apparently spent more time driving *through* the community and less time serving *with* and *within* the immediate community. It was also evident upon my arrival that a generation of young adults was missing, leaving an aging congregation wondering why they would choose to worship elsewhere or not at all. During a conversation in which some of the older members expressed relevant concerns about the missing "young people" and shared several reasons why they believed this generation was not attending their church, some of them refused to accept any responsibility for creating and promoting a church environment that repelled rather than attracted young adults and young families.

A primary reason for this generation's absence—and the primary cause of my increasing dissatisfaction—was the unwavering commitment many of the more influential leaders had to the church's past. This attitude and relative practices were reminiscent of the common thread of dying churches described by Thom Rainer in his book *Autopsy of a Deceased Church*. He writes, "The most common thread of our autopsies was that the deceased churches lived for a long time with the past as hero. They held on more tightly with each progressive year. They often clung to things of the past with desperation and fear. And when any internal or external force tried to change the past, they responded with anger and resolution: We will die before we change. And they did. Hear me clearly: these churches were not hanging on to biblical truths. They were not clinging to clear Christian morality. They were not fighting for primary doctrines, secondary doctrines, or even tertiary doctrines. As a matter of fact, they were not fighting for doctrines at all. They were fighting for the past. The good old days. The way it used to be."[6] To be clear, there was plenty to appreciate and celebrate about this church's past. We were also grateful for the pastors and numerous people who served faithfully over the years in shaping their very meaningful history. The problem was intentionally ignoring their changing community while insisting on operating according to the practices of the past that were unattractive to many current and prospective members, especially those identified as young adults.

Recognizing how deeply entrenched many of the leaders and members were in their fight to hold onto and live in the past, I prayed for a way to lead them in developing a new perspective of both their past and their future. My efforts began with something I read in the book *Finding Our Story: Narrative Leadership and Congregational Change*. Writing about how stories work, Gil Rendle writes, "Give people facts (persuasive leadership engaging reason), and the conversation stumbles over agreement or disputation of the facts. Give people a good story, a bold story, and the conversation intuitively leaps ahead to action, allowing people

---

[6] Thom Rainer, *Autopsy of a Deceased Church: 12 Ways to Keep Yours Alive* (Nashville: B&H Publishing Group 2014), 18.

to *know* and to give meaning to the action."[7] If I was going to succeed in leading them in developing a bold new story, I needed to resist communicating the obvious facts contributing to both a continual decrease in attendance and an ineffective presence in the community. Instead, I believed my best approach was to lead the church out of its weak story that was the product of its remembered past and into its new story. In doing so, the words of Harvard professor Howard Gardner were a constant reminder of the challenge I was facing:

> The audience is not simply a blank slate, however, waiting for the first, or for the best, story to be etched on its virginal tablet. Rather, audience members come equipped with many stories that have already been told and retold in their homes, their societies and their domains. The stories of the leader—be they traditional or novel—must compete with many other extant stories; and if the new stories are to succeed, they must transplant, suppress, compliment, or in some measure outweigh the earlier stories, as well as contemporary oppositional counter stories.[8]

Using a combination of two developmental constructs—(1) William Isaacs's dialogue map that moves groups through the four

---

[7] Gil Rendle, "Narrative Leadership and Renewed Congregational Identity," in *Finding Our Story: Narrative Leadership and Congregational Change*, ed. Larry Golemon (Lanham, MD: Rowman & Littlefield, 2010), 25.

[8] Howard Gardner, *Leading Minds: An Anatomy of Leadership* (New York: Basic Books, 1995), 13.

stages of politeness, breakdown, inquiry, and flow and (2) Lawrence Porter and Bernard Mohr's four-stage process of group development including forming, storming, norming, and performing—I attempted to lead the congregation to their new story. Rendle identifies these constructs in tandem as "Politeness and Forming, Breakdown and Storming, Inquiry and Norming, and Flow and Performing."[9]

## STAGE 1: POLITENESS AND FORMING

In the development of relationships, politeness and forming characterize the initial stage of getting to know another person. In marriage, it is courtship. Politeness and forming are the heart of the common advice to pastors to not change anything for a year until they know the people and the congregation. Developmentally, the group question being addressed in this earliest stage of community is, "Do we belong together?" What is being tested is whether the "you" and the "I" have enough similarities to allow us to remain together. Will we understand and appreciate one another? Can I trust you with me? Can you appreciate me without needing me to change?[10]

This period of the pastor-congregation relationship is commonly known as the honeymoon phase during which, as mentioned above,

---

[9] Rendle, *Narrative Leadership*, 32–38.

[10] Ibid.

pastors know it is a bad idea to make any significant changes during the first year of the relationship. Experienced pastors may have learned this from trial and error while first-time pastors are often informed of this by their pastors and mentors when considering assuming a pastoral post. Regardless of how the pastor learns this lesson, the reality is that each of us deals with the temptation to do the opposite. Having been called to lead our respective congregations, we see this tradition as a hindrance to immediately displaying pastoral leadership abilities when, in fact, impatiently making unwanted changes is likely to become an even bigger hindrance and further delay necessary changes.

This stage is also a period when both pastor and people attempt to understand one another through the sharing of stories while also evaluating their ability to effectively coexist in a shared space. Congregations like the one I inherited often stick to initially telling weak stories that are the products of a remembered past when pews were filled and ministry programs were plenty. Weak stories are not *bad* stories. They are comfortable stories that were likely chosen in the past to reduce the risk of disrupting established church harmonies. During my first year with this church, the weak stories of a treasured past were shared both in an introductory manner and as a means of conveying to me the desired direction in which they wanted me to lead them. It was later confirmed by the continual telling of these weak stories that any chance I had of successfully providing this congregation with authentic pastoral leadership hinged on my willingness to help them cling to their past by duplicating "the good old days" that were culturally irrelevant within the current community. Though I missed the signals at the time, there was no way some of the more influential, past-focused members of this congregation would appreciate and accept me as my authentic self.

## STAGE 2: BREAKDOWN AND STORMING

> Breakdown and storming characterize the stage at which narrative leadership—as distinct from storytelling—first kicks in. In the dynamics of group development, the central question shifts from "Do we belong together?" to "Who's in control?" Is there only one way for the congregation to tell its story here, or will people allow their leaders to tell it in a way that might be riskier and less comfortable?[11]

This is the stage that moves us from shared monologues to dialogue, in which the leader introduces ways and opportunities for the congregation to create a new story to live by. This journey from a weak and safe story into a better, bolder story begins with prayerfully engaging in a conversation about the identity of the congregation. The mistake that pastors commonly make in this stage is beginning the conversation with evaluative statements about what is wrong with the church and immediately offering solutions with very little, if any, input from the congregation.

The risk to pastoral leadership in this stage comes with the breaking and storming that are vital to the transition to a new identity and story. In my case, and reminiscent of the story of Paul and Silas in Acts 16, this is where the foundation was shaken beneath the feet of the captives. However, many merely focused on the

---

[11] Rendle, *Narrative Leadership*, 33–34.

shaking and completely missed the loosening of chains and the opening of doors. Efforts to lead change were met with resistance and at times even anger whenever those efforts felt as if they were designed to loosen the tradition-driven death grip on the past.

Gaining a balcony perspective during this stage was a tremendous help in that it led me in identifying congregational behaviors similar to those described by Larry Osborne in his writing on being "Flock Focused"[12] where he identifies the differences between struggling sheep and infectious sheep. Struggling sheep, although many do not always seem to put up much of a fight against their wrongdoings, really want things to be different. They want to do and be better but continue to lose more spiritual battles than they win. They keep trying. They keep serving. They keep praying and confessing with the hope of learning to live better and grow stronger in their faith. Infectious sheep, on the other hand, have given up in the battle. They have given in to their temptations. Instead of struggling and fighting against their wrongs, they have engaged in the practice of defending their sins and categorizing them as no big deal to God and others. The struggling sheep need our help. The infectious sheep need to be quarantined.

I inherited quite a few more struggling sheep than infectious sheep, and over time, the church began attracting community members that fit well into the struggling-sheep category. Unfortunately, the infectious-sheep minority possessed and wielded a great deal of negative influence within the church and engaged in tactics and behaviors that gradually increased their support by infecting struggling sheep or discouraging many of them, ultimately

---

[12] Larry Osborne, *Lead Like a Shepherd: The Secret to Leading Well* (Nashville: Thomas Nelson, 2018), 89–98.

leading to their departure. Many of the struggling sheep, however, remained with us and continued to faithfully fight for their personal spiritual growth as well as that of the church and community. With their support, we continued to have meaningful conversations and wrestle with our identity—with who we were at that particular time so we could move forward in creating a new and bolder story. During our conversations, the vision God had given me for this church began taking shape as we focused our efforts on establishing a better relationship with the immediate community while transitioning into the next phase of inquiry and norming.

## STAGE 3: INQUIRY AND NORMING

At the third stage of the development of the relationship and the story of the congregation, the "new" is created. In terms of group life, the initial questions, "Do we belong together?" and "Who is in charge?" have now moved on to the third question of "Okay, now that we see things differently, how will we move ahead?" This is the norming stage, because new agreements, or norms, about what is important and how the congregation will behave are being established, based on what was learned in the first two stages.[13]

As the church began attracting more members who lived in the immediate community, it became increasingly clear that our community involvement was exactly where God wanted us to focus

---

[13] Rendle, *Narrative Leadership*, 35.

our energy and resources. Although some in leadership seemed to increase their grip on the past, we were generally beginning to see things differently while experiencing a newfound joy beyond the walls of the church. We learned during this stage that our increasing growth did not eliminate the need for the occasional hard and often messy conversations that were productive only when we engaged in David Bohm's reflective dialogue where the new always comes from the speaking and the listening involved in the dialogue.[14] In other words, we were engaging in shared dialogue during which we were learning from what each of us was offering instead of challenging each other's comments and suggestions.

Much of our success was the result of the work of our youth and young adult minister and his wife. Their love, creativity, and tireless service to our community attracted entire families to our church. Through trips for children, community concerts, relevant Bible studies, and other creative activities, this couple played a major part in our efforts to lead community residents to life-changing faith in Jesus Christ. We also participated with community groups and partnered with community activists in addressing numerous issues associated with the ongoing efforts to gentrify our community. Problems within the community presented us with opportunities to provide a Christian perspective and continually remind residents and local business owners of God's life-giving and life-changing presence and power.

Although this stage of inquiry and norming was filled with the hope of collectively creating a new story for the church to live by, this was also a period of revelation during which the infectious sheep confirmed their deep-seated desire to move backward instead

---

[14] David Bohm, *On Dialogue* (London: Routledge, 1996), 2.

of forward. As mentioned before, the congregation was growing relationally both inside and outside the walls of the church, which led to increased membership and attendance stemming mostly from the immediate community. But since some of the newcomers arrived bringing with them the weight of things like poverty, drug and alcohol addiction, homosexuality, teenage pregnancy and parenting, limited education, and homelessness, some of the "church elite" displayed a noticeably superficial acceptance of them that impaired our church-community relationship and hindered our progress in creating our new story.

## STAGE 4: FLOW AND PERFORMING

> This final stage of flow and performing is the arena of maturity where a new authenticity of dialogue and community is lived out. Finding the right story, the bold and faithful story, can provide life and purpose for a congregation over an extended period.[15]

Unfortunately, my relationship with this church never reached stage 4 as I realized that unless I made some personal behavioral changes and began providing inauthentic leadership, we were not going to experience the envisioned period of congregational life and purpose found in a new, bold, and faithful story.

While still navigating the inquiry and norming of stage 3, I found myself at a familiar place for pastors where it appeared that the only solution to maintaining congregational momentum was to

---

[15] Rendle, *Narrative Leadership*, 36–37.

remove leaders who were fully committed to purposely hindering our growth and progression. Even some who were fully engaged in our initial efforts had, by this time, regressed into a belief that ministry effectiveness could only be realized by replicating the story of the past instead of following God into creating a new future story. They worked hard to convince others of this belief by sowing seeds of doubt throughout the congregation, particularly related to my leadership skills and abilities. I was not that concerned about this backward-focused group achieving success in influencing other members to join them. I was ultimately concerned about new and potential followers of Christ currently attending our church being discouraged by witnessing behaviors and hearing comments that should never be exhibited and expressed by believers, especially those in leadership positions. As I considered strategies for removing specific leaders and the inevitable tension and conflict associated with such a move, I recalled a helpful story I once read. In fact, it was the very last paragraph of the story that made the biggest impact and is why I remembered it.

> The Philadelphia economy was struggling in the 1750's, and no one could comprehend why. Other cities in Colonial America—especially Boston and New York—were growing. It's not that life was wretched in the City of Brotherly Love; it was just vaguely unpleasant, and no one could put his finger on what was wrong. No one, that is, except Benjamin Franklin.
>
> When economies are struggling, big fixes are often tempting. The city leaders in Philadelphia

could have tried a number of expensive solutions. They could have built more wharves and warehouses to increase trade. They could have improved the roads leading to the city or hired a full-time militia to increase security. Benjamin Franklin made a small and rather curious recommendation: hire some street sweepers.

Franklin observed a great deal of dust swirling around the streets of the commercial district in Philadelphia. When the dust got bad, two things happened: the local shopkeepers kept their doors closed, and people sought the comfort of home rather than the irritation of the streets. When a few people were paid to keep the streets as dust-free as possible, people returned to the commercial district, and business picked up. "Some may think these trifling matters not worth minding," Franklin would later write in his autobiography. Dust in one person's eyes, admittedly, is an inconvenience. Dust in everyone's eyes, he argued, could seriously hamper a city's economic and social vitality. "Human happiness," Franklin continued, "is produced not so much by great pieces of good fortune that seldom happen, as by little advantages that occur every day."

Shepherd leaders are certainly wise to seize the "great pieces of good fortune that seldom happen." However, it's a foolish leader that lets a thousand and one small opportunities for improvement slip away while pinning all hopes on another big event.

Why? Because a better life for your followers is often a product of the "little advantages that occur every day." At times the advantage is gained by adding something beneficial. More often, as in Franklin's case, it's gained by removing something irritating.[16]

The dust of tradition and desired regression had become an increasing irritant that began to impact relationships both in the church and community. Like the people in the story who avoided the irritation of the streets, frustrated church members chose to avoid the irritants in the church by staying home or attending elsewhere. Admittedly, this dust also began to significantly impact my desire to serve as the pastor of this church.

## ■ RESIGNATION

With prayerful consideration and after having received extensive pastoral counsel and guidance, it came as a surprise to several members of the boards of deacons and trustees when I submitted to them my letter of resignation, giving them the required sixty-day notice. As we discussed why I had made this decision, the initial response of the majority in attendance was to consider what could be done to repair our relationship within the next sixty days. There were questions about whether more pay and/or pastoral authority would lead to reconciliation. I explained during our discussion that I was not using my resignation as a negotiation tactic and would not be entertaining any conversations pertaining to that assumption.

---

[16] Blaine McCormick and David Davenport, *Shepherd Leadership: Wisdom for Leaders from Psalm 23* (San Francisco: Jossey-Bass, 2003), 79–80.

As I clearly explained to them on that very memorable evening, I knew God sent me to this church to lead them in whichever way He directed, and I was very appreciative to have been given the opportunity to do so. However, I was sure that the only way to satisfy them was to deny my authentic self and serve in that capacity as someone other than who God made and called me to be.

According to the church's constitution and by-laws, a meeting with the board of deacons was required prior to announcing my resignation to the church body. At this meeting, held exactly one week after submitting my resignation, it was obvious that the deacons who were more than happy to see me leave had influenced some of my supportive deacons to join them in what became the beginning of a series of attempts to tarnish my reputation as much as possible before I officially left the church. Some who were initially interested in exploring options for me to remain and continue serving as their pastor were, just seven days later, agreeing with leading deacons who were now accusing me of misleading the congregation biblically and preaching divisive sermons. Interestingly, the sermon they pointed to specifically was a recent one about deacons from the sixth chapter of the book of Acts. As evidence of the leading deacons' negative influence, one of the previously supportive deacons who initially agreed with the divisive sermon accusation later admitted that he had not heard the sermon in question prior to this meeting and was wrong in blindly supporting those making the false accusations. Some gave me their complete support while others remained fearfully silent.

During this meeting, I presented the deacons with my preaching plan that would gradually transfer this responsibility to the associate minister who was completely capable of fulfilling this role and who had established meaningful relationships with the congregation and community through his previously mentioned work primarily with our youth and young adult population. Obviously planned and agreed upon by a faction of the deacon board prior to the meeting, I was told in no uncertain terms that this group was prohibiting me from preaching any more sermons at this church. I adjourned the meeting immediately after making those in the room aware of their ill-perceived authority and inability to carry out their intentions.

Aware that word of my resignation was quickly spreading, I planned to make the official announcement to the congregation following the upcoming Sunday service. During the time between the Wednesday night deacons' meeting and the following Sunday announcement, I prayerfully considered preaching but ultimately decided to follow God's clearly communicated desire for me to take the high road by minimizing the inevitable attempts by certain deacons and trustees to create conflict and congregational disunity. As planned, I made my resignation announcement to the congregation and laid out some of the steps involved in my departure including the deacons' desire for me to cease all preaching at this church. As expected, many in attendance were disappointed and saddened by my decision. However, many of the leaders and members who witnessed the continual mistreatment of the pastor by specific leaders and their minions expressed their understanding and support of my decision to leave.

Inevitably, my resignation exposed the ungodly leadership practices of certain deacons and trustees who immediately began engaging in a series of evil and unnecessary actions and behaviors, especially since I had decided not to preach as part of my goal of leaving as nonconfrontationally as possible. Instead of behaving respectfully and cordially during my final weeks or paying me for this period of time and severing ties immediately as I had previously suggested, they started sending emails and text messages to leaders and members that were designed to discredit me and childishly refused to speak to me or relate to me in any form during worship services and other gatherings. In an unexpected move, they arranged to have the locks changed on my office door while knowing I was away caring for a dying friend and her family.

After I arranged to collect my belongings and leave prior to the original target date, their next move was an attempt to withhold my final check until I signed a document that would prevent me from all future personal communication with members of the church, prohibit me from ever visiting or attending the church (as if I had any desire to do so), and prevent me from sharing the truth about their recent actions and behavior. In response, I told them that my attorney, who I was currently speaking with by phone, advised me to leave if I did not have my check within the next ten minutes and for them to expect to hear from her sometime afterward. The check was handed to me within five minutes.

I later learned of their final move to discredit me and save face with the remaining congregants by holding a closed meeting where they actually locked the parking lot gate and would not allow attendees to leave without returning a multipage document outlining their accusations about me. Their secrecy was to ensure that I did not obtain a copy of this document. Thanks to friends who opposed their efforts, I received the complete packet of information they used in this meeting.

I had resigned from churches before this experience but never expected to find myself in a situation that can only be described as one of those things that "only happens to other people." While prayerfully trying to understand how so-called church leaders could be so intentionally hurtful and go to extensive lengths in justifying their ungodly practices, I found solace in the wisdom of my pastor, Dr. Joseph A. Keaton, who explained to me that the only way for this group to maintain their ill-gotten authority and reckless congregational influence was to create their version of how our relationship would end. His simple yet profound advice was to just let them do it and let God deal with them. His guidance confirmed the words of Robert Dale in his writing about spiritual disciplines for leaders: "Enlist a spiritual director. A mature leader with a disciplined devotional life and the gift of sensitivity offers the resource of friendly guidance."[17]

My decision to resign and the ensuing experiences created feelings of anxiety and occasional moments of doubt that were always subdued by reading and reflecting on two biblical passages from Genesis and Matthew:

> So God created mankind in his own image, in the image of God he created them; male and female he created them.[18]

> You are the light of the world. A town built on a hill cannot be hidden. Neither do people light a lamp and put it under a bowl. Instead they put it on its stand, and it gives light to everyone in the house. In the same way, let your light shine before others,

---

[17] Robert Dale, *Pastoral Leadership* (Nashville: Abingdon Press, 1986), 192.
[18] Gen. 1:27.

that they may see your good deeds and glorify your
Father in heaven.[19]

These words provided the clarity and confidence I needed
to continue walking authentically in God's will during the most
difficult experience of my pastoral career. In doing so faithfully,
I discovered my desire and calling to use my experience as a
springboard into researching the topic of "Maintaining Pastoral
Authenticity through Resignation and Termination" by speaking
extensively to other pastors with similar experiences, leading to the
development of this project. Details of these conversations including
helpful insights for others will be presented in chapter 3.

---

[19] Matt. 5:14–16.

# CHAPTER 2

# JOB'S CONSTANT NATURE

When addressing pastoral authenticity from a biblical/theological perspective, one would expect the focus to center on biblical characters who assumed pastoral or pseudo-pastoral roles. Apostle Paul is certainly a consideration along with the twelve disciples who, according to the book of Acts, selected deacons in order to give their attention to prayer and the ministry of the Word. However, after considering these and others in the Bible who possessed and displayed qualifying leadership traits, I was led by the Holy Spirit to use Job as my central biblical/theological character. While Job did not assume a pastoral role, his ability to maintain his spiritual and relational authenticity through significant life changes speaks directly to this project and provides additional opportunities to focus on authenticity from a broader perspective rather than solely from a pastor-specific point of view. Job is also ideal for this project because of his existing character traits identified prior to Satan's interference.

These will be addressed at length in this chapter. It is therefore presupposed that those who will benefit most from this project are pastors who have already established an existing habit of serving with the utmost integrity at the time they began experiencing hardships stemming from congregational hostility.

The relevance of Job's story to that of a pastor's can be heard in the sentiment that life is not just difficult, it is downright unfair. Difficulties are expected, especially as our responsibilities multiply. Job's ten children, numerous servants, and hundreds of animals would certainly have come with their respective difficulties. Likewise, there are inherent difficulties found in sermon preparation, counseling, visiting the sick, and church meetings—all while taking care of a family. These difficulties can rightly be summed up as coming with the territory. Jesus said in Luke 12, "From everyone who has been given much, much will be demanded; and from the one who has been entrusted with much, much more will be asked."[20] While being given and entrusted with much is a true blessing from God, correctly managing it all can become quite difficult, especially when these difficulties lead to undeserved suffering.

In his introduction of Job in his paraphrase of the Old Testament, Eugene Petersen says,

> It is not only because Job suffered that he is important to us. It is because he suffered in the same ways that we suffer—in the vital areas of family, personal health, and material things. Job is also important to us because he searchingly questioned and boldly protested his suffering. Indeed, he

---

[20] Lk. 12:48.

went "to the top" with his questions. It is not the suffering that troubles us. It is undeserved suffering. Almost all of us in our years of growing up have the experience of disobeying our parents and getting punished for it. When that discipline was connected to wrongdoing, it had a certain sense of justice to it: *When we do wrong, we get punished.*

One of the surprises as we get older, however, is that we come to see that there is no real correlation between the amount of wrong we commit and the amount of pain we experience. An even larger surprise is that very often there is something quite the opposite: We do right and get knocked down. We do the best we are capable of doing, and just as we are reaching out to receive our reward we are hit from the blind side and sent reeling.[21]

This certainly describes Job's life—not just difficult, but unfair. Being blindsided with undeserved suffering put Job's faith, integrity, and authenticity to the test. There are undoubtedly many pastors with the same testimony.

While speaking to a colleague recently about this project, he identified his current standing as the pastor of his church as "barely hanging on" and pointed to the undeserved suffering he endures almost weekly as the basis for this description of his place in ministry. By no means is this friend perfect, nor would he ever profess to be. But in his twenty-plus years as a pastor, I have always

---

[21] Eugene H. Petersen, "Introduction to Job," from *The Message* (Colorado Springs: NavPress, 2002), 839.

known him as a man of impeccable integrity. Ironically, he felt as though the undeserved suffering he experienced intensified with every step he took in the right direction and with every decision he made in accordance with God's will.

He then raised an interesting question: why would God create us in His image, call us to lead His people, and allow us to be treated so unfairly and undeservingly? As we pondered that thought, we considered that the answer is found somewhere in the fact that God trusted Job to endure his suffering and must likewise trust pastors. After all, it was God who permitted Satan to torment Job, initially offering Job up without provocation from Satan. As Paul says to the church in Corinth, "And God is faithful; he will not let you be tempted beyond what you can bear. But when you are tempted, he will also provide a way out so that you can endure."[22] My friend inserted relative to Job's experience and Paul's statement to the church in Corinth that it is not that there is a lack of trusting God in these moments. It is the verbal and emotional beating taken while waiting for Him to provide a way out that wears on his faith and is the reason he is considering leaving his church and possibly the pastorate.

Because a significant part of Job's story focuses on his response to loss and affliction, his experience is viewed by many as one of character development. However, I believe a stronger argument can be made for this being a story of *maintaining* one's character and authenticity as Job is guided throughout his story by a preexisting noble character in what can be described as the most extreme circumstances. Prior to Satan's appearance, the Bible introduces Job as a man who was blameless and upright, one who feared God

---

[22] 1 Cor. 10:13.

and shunned evil. In this descriptive introduction, according to Christopher Ash, "We are told four things about Job: his integrity, his treatment of others, his religion, and his morality. These four things tell us, not what Job was from time to time or occasionally, but his constant nature."[23] Job's constant, unchanging nature speaks not only of his response to severe physical and emotional affliction but also reveals who he was prior to his hardships. While his experience would have certainly impacted his spiritual development, it primarily revealed an already existing nature—*integrity, treatment of others, religion,* and *morality*—that allowed him to persevere while also setting an example for us to follow.

## ■ INTEGRITY

The New International Version (NIV) of the Bible tells us that Job was *blameless,* which is a more appropriate translation than the use of *perfect* in the King James Version of the Bible. Any notion that this meant he was sinless is later dismissed by Job himself when he speaks of "the sins of my youth"[24] and again when Job says to God, "Surely then you will count my steps but not keep track of my sin."[25] This word basically speaks of sincerity, genuineness, and authenticity, which all point to the necessary character trait of integrity. Throughout Job's story, we get to witness a display of integrity, particularly during his increasingly intensifying dialogue with his friends Eliphaz, Bildad, and Zophar. While he could have taken advantage of opportunities to blame others for his suffering,

---

[23] Christopher Ash, *Job: The Wisdom of the Cross* (Wheaton, IL., 2014), 31.
[24] Job 13:26.
[25] Job 14:16.

Job's integrity forced him to look within himself and acknowledge his own deficiencies instead of looking outside himself to justify them.

In their book *Becoming a Person of Influence: How to Positively Impact the Lives of Others*, John Maxwell and Jim Dornan label integrity as an inside job and give three helpful truths about integrity that often go against common thinking:

## INTEGRITY IS NOT DETERMINED BY CIRCUMSTANCES

> Some psychologists and sociologists today tell us that many people of poor character would not be the way they are if only they had grown up in a different environment. Now, it's true that our upbringing and circumstances affect who we are, especially when we are young. But the older we are, the greater number of choices we make—for good or bad. Two people can grow up in the same environment, even in the same household, and one will have integrity and the other won't. Ultimately, you are responsible for your choices. Your circumstances are as responsible for your character as a mirror is for your looks. What you see only reflects what you are.[26]

An example of the effect one's circumstances have on their character can be found by comparing Job's response to ruin to that of his wife. Her response leads one to believe she may have been an ungrateful

[26] John C. Maxwell and Jim Dornan, *Becoming a Person of Influence: How to Positively Impact the Lives of Others* (Nashville: Thomas Nelson, 1997), 22.

and unfaithful woman. I would argue otherwise. Job's success as a businessman, his relationship with God, and the relationships their children had with one another indicate that Job would likely have selected a wife who fits the description of a wife with the noble character found in Proverbs 31. It was not until Satan was granted access into their lives that it appeared she may have lacked the same level of integrity and spiritual maturity as her husband. While Job is sitting in ashes scraping his sores with a piece of broken pottery, his wife pleads with him, "Are you still maintaining your integrity? Curse God and die!"[27] Again, some allowances must be made on her behalf considering that she had also recently suffered significant life-changing losses. She lost her children and her wealth, and it may appear to her at that moment that her husband, whom she loves dearly, may also be in jeopardy of losing his life. One could argue that any emotionally distraught person might react as she did. However, Job's reaction reflects the very behavior his wife addresses in her question to him.

Although their shared circumstances caused her to abandon her own integrity, Job accepted his suffering as God's will by replying, "Shall we accept good from God and not trouble?"[28] Reflected in his question is Job's willingness and ability to see the blessings of the past as motivation to maintain his integrity and his faith in God. According to Rawlinson, "He accepts both prosperity and affliction as coming from God and expresses himself as willing to submit to his will. But he has, perhaps, scarcely attained the conviction that whatever God sends to his faithful servants is always that which is

---

[27] Job 2:9.

[28] Job 2:10.

best for them—that afflictions, in fact, are blessings in disguise, and ought to be received with gratitude, not murmuring."[29]

Evidence of integrity not being determined by circumstances can also be seen by observing the behaviors of some pastors who have a lifetime of church experience and others who came to Christ and the pastorate much later in life. It may be reasonable to assume that those who have spent much more time serving Christ in the church and community would be less susceptible to the temptation of compromising their integrity. But experience has proven that pastors from different backgrounds—one raised in the church and another coming to Christ much later in life—who were guided by the same mentors and served in similar pastoral roles can have completely differing views on integrity. As stated by Maxwell and Dornan, "Two people can grow up in the same environment ... and one will have integrity and the other won't."[30]

Pastoral integrity and authenticity are often challenged during the course of one's career by circumstances arising mainly from within the walls of the church, and each pastor must choose daily how to respond—hopefully with integrity—to those challenging circumstances. In those instances, it would be helpful to remember the words of Paul to the Philippians: "Do not be anxious about anything, but in every situation, by prayer and petition, with thanksgiving, present your requests to God. And the peace of God, which transcends all understanding, will guard your hearts

---

[29] G. Rawlinson, "Job," in *The Pulpit Commentary, Volume 7: Ezra, Nehemiah, Esther & Job*, ed. H.D.M. Spence and Joseph S. Exell (Peabody, MA: Hendrickson, 1985), 35.

[30] Maxwell and Dornan, *Becoming a Person of Influence*, 22.

and your minds in Christ Jesus."[31] Regardless of past or existing circumstances, placing everything into God's hands in prayer will not only bring one peace but will also lead one to act with integrity.

## INTEGRITY IS NOT BASED ON CREDENTIALS

In ancient times, brick makers, engravers, and other artisans used a symbol to mark the things they created to show that they were the makers. The symbol that each one used was his "character." The value of the work was in proportion to the skill with which the object was made. And only if the quality of the work was high was the character esteemed. In other words, the quality of the person and his work gave value to his credentials. If the work was good, so was the character. If it was bad, then the character was viewed as poor.

The same is true today. Character comes from who we are. But some like to be judged not by who they are but by the titles they have earned or the position they hold regardless of the nature of their character. Their desire is to influence others by the weight of their credentials rather than the strength of their character. But credentials can never accomplish what character can. Look at some differences between the two:

| Credentials | Character |
| --- | --- |
| Are transient | Is permanent |
| Turn the focus to rights | Keeps the focus on responsibilities |

---

[31] Phil. 4:6–7.

| | |
|---|---|
| Add value to only one person | Adds value to many people |
| Look to past accomplishments | Builds a legacy for the future |
| Often evoke jealousy in others | Generates respect and integrity |
| Can only get you in the door | Keeps you there[32] |

While there is nothing inherently wrong with possessing certain credentials, the previous statement referring to pastors whose desire is to influence others by the weight of their credentials rather than the strength of their character points to the potential for a much larger problem within the body of Christ. We are told in the book of 1 John, "Do not love the world or anything in the world. If anyone loves the world, love for the Father is not in them. For everything in the world—the lust of the flesh, the lust of the eyes, and the pride of life—comes not from the Father but from the world. The world and its desires pass away, but whoever does the will of God lives forever."[33] A brief but helpful summary of these verses is found in *The Pulpit Commentary*: "The duty of loving in one direction must involve the corresponding duty of not loving in an opposite and alien direction."[34] To give external credentials a place of significant precedence over internal character in the performance of pastoral duties will eventually lead to loving in the wrong direction and ultimately have a negative impact on pastoral leadership and congregational care.

Additionally, placing inappropriate importance on credentials

---

[32] Maxwell and Dornan, *Becoming a Person of Influence*, 23.

[33] 1 John 2:15–17.

[34] C. Clemance, "The Epistles of St. John," in *The Pulpit Commentary, Volume 22: Epistles of Peter, John & Jude. The Revelation*, ed. H.D.M. Spence and Joseph S. Exell (Peabody, MA: Hendrickson, 1985), 35.

can develop certain expectations a pastor may have relative to how they are to be treated, addressed, and sometimes revered. Reserved parking spaces, special seating, and public acknowledgment of attendance at services and events are just a few things that come into play for a pastor who values credentials and status over character. It must be noted here that most of the pastors I have encountered who harbor these credentials-driven expectations are really good people, which speaks of how easily even the best of God's servants can be hindered by "the sin that so easily entangles."[35]

One such pastor recalled attending a church conference for pastors many years ago that included a public worship service. As the service commenced, the pastors were lined up single file and led into the worship center where a staff pastor from the host church guided each of them into a seating area reserved for attending pastors. When he approached the staff pastor fully expecting to follow everyone else into the reserved area, he was instead directed to find a seat in an already populated and obscure area of the worship center. By the time he found a seat, he felt angry, offended, and embarrassed as others watched and wondered why he was not allowed to sit with the other pastors. Unfortunately, his emotions prevented him from engaging in worship and focusing on the preacher's message.

He did, however, have a friend who moved from the reserved section and, much like Job's friends, sat quietly with him throughout the service. While his friend would have been justified in convicting him by pointing out how his credentials-over-character mentality and expectations played a major part in his anger, he did none of that. Instead, he left his well-deserved position in the reserved

---

[35] Heb. 12:1.

section and put the angry pastor's needs before his own. In the end, he realized that although the staff pastor did not allow him access into the area of honor, it was his credentials-driven expectations that were responsible for his feelings and inappropriate response, which he later discovered had negatively influenced others who witnessed his behavior. No number of titles, degrees, offices, designations, awards, licenses, or other credentials can substitute for basic integrity when it comes to the power of influencing others.

## INTEGRITY IS NOT TO BE CONFUSED WITH REPUTATION

One of the reasons it is easy to confuse integrity with reputation is that many of us misunderstand or are completely ignorant of how much control we have concerning our own reputations. Truth is, we never have control over our reputations, only influence. Reputations represent "the collective mental construct everyone *but* you shares *about* you, a construct based partially on your own actions but also on the perceptions others have about others' perceptions of your actions."[36] This misunderstanding may also lead to the mistake of emphasizing reputation over character and integrity. Listen to what William Hersey Davis has to say about the difference between character and its shadow, reputation:

---

[36] Alex Lickerman, "The Value of a Good Reputation: Why We Should Care About How Others Perceive Us," *Psychology Today*, (April 2010), accessed October 3, 2019, https://www.psychologytoday.com/us/blog/happiness-in-world/201004/the-value-good-reputation.

The circumstances amid which you live determine your reputation …

the truth you believe determines your character …

Reputation is what you are supposed to be;

character is what you are …

Reputation is the photograph;

character is the face …

Reputation comes over one from without;

character grows from within …

Reputation is what you have when you come to a new community;

character is what you have when you go away.

Your reputation is made in a moment;

your character is built in a lifetime …

Your reputation is learned in an hour;

your character does not come to light for a year …

Reputation grows like a mushroom;

character lasts like eternity …

Reputation makes you rich or makes you poor;

character makes you happy or makes you miserable …

Reputation is what men say about you on your tombstone;

character is what the angels say about you before the throne of God.

Certainly, a good reputation is valuable. King Solomon of ancient Israel stated, "A good name is more desirable than great riches." But a good reputation exists because it is a reflection of a person's character. If a good reputation is like gold, then having integrity is like owning the mine. Worry less about what others think, and give more attention to your inner character.[37]

Another useful method of comprehending Job's integrity may be to contrast it with that of the Pharisees in the New Testament—those who certainly confused integrity with reputation. These were men who mastered the art of pretending to be someone externally that differed from who they were internally. This behavior is described in 2 Timothy as "having a form of godliness but denying its power."[38] Jesus even addressed this by saying to the Pharisees, "You hypocrites! Isaiah was right when he prophesied about you: These people honor me with their lips, but their hearts are far from me. They worship me in vain; their teachings are merely human rules."[39] Job's godly appearance and his speech were an accurate reflection of the genuine godliness in his heart whereas the appearance and speech of the Pharisees reflected a heart filled with traditionalism and hypocrisy. It is imperative that pastoral integrity and authenticity are displayed in such a way that when others hear our words and watch our deeds, they also see an accurate reflection of the love of Christ in our hearts.

---

[37] Maxwell and Dornan, *Becoming a Person of Influence*, 23–24.

[38] 2 Tim. 3:5.

[39] Matt. 15:7–9.

## ▪ TREATMENT OF OTHERS

The reference to Job being *upright* speaks of one with an impeccable character who treated others with the utmost respect. The remarkable number of possessions Job had amassed points to his business dealing where his uprightness would have been evident. Wool from his seven thousand sheep would have been sold or woven into garments that would have also been sold or given to those in need. Many of Job's three thousand camels would have been for hire and used in caravans. His one thousand oxen were used to plow his fields and prepare the soil for the sewing and harvesting of an abundance of food. Job's life as a well-respected businessman would have put him in contact with others whom he treated fairly. This upright treatment of others is reflected in Job's soliloquy in chapter 31:

> Did not he who made me in the womb make them?
> Did not the same one form us both within our
> mothers? If I have denied the desires of the poor
> or let the eyes of the widow grow weary, if I have
> kept my bread to myself, not sharing it with the
> fatherless—but from my youth I reared them as
> a father would, and from my birth I guided the
> widow—if I have seen anyone perishing for lack of
> clothing, or the needy without garments, and their
> hearts did not bless me for warming them with
> the fleece from my sheep, if I have raised my hand
> against the fatherless, knowing that I had influence
> in court, then let my arm fall from the shoulder, let it
> be broken off at the joint. For I dreaded destruction

from God and for fear of his splendor I could not
do such things.[40]

The good deeds Job presents on his own behalf as evidence of the way he treated others are ordinary things that can be accomplished by good people today. Though he displayed extraordinary discipline throughout his ordeal, it was the simple acts of kindness that he referred to in pleading his case.

A word of caution is appropriate relative to the treatment of others as a pastor—do not forget about your treatment of those in your own home. Gary Preston sheds some insight on this topic in his book *Pastors in Pain: How to Grow in Times of Conflict*. After having been forced out of the pastorate prematurely by the church board and experiencing unemployment firsthand, Gary writes, "For the first week I felt overcome by low-grade depression and helplessness. With little or no provocation, I would shout at our children or snap at my wife. Some days I just sat paralyzed in my living room chair, barely able to answer the phone."[41] While he later commends his wife for her support and patience during their unsettling times, Preston implies that the unprovoked lashing out at their children was due in part to his refusal to acknowledge the impact this loss had on them. Being young, his children could not understand why they could not attend their church anymore, why they could not sing in the choir with their friends, and why they could not attend church summer camp with other families. Knowing that a job loss can too often result in serious family problems including divorce, Preston and his

---

[40] Job 31:15–23.

[41] Gary Preston, *Pastors in Pain: How to Grow in Times of Conflict* (Grand Rapids, MI: BakerBooks 1999), 20.

wife used it to pull their family together, even allowing their children to help them deal with their grief.

As previously mentioned, although I left my former church voluntarily, I still struggled with some of the same things as Gary Preston (and so many others) because of the intensity and volume of deacon-driven church conflict involved in my departure. Impatience, a short temper, abrupt mood swings, and other emotions and reactions stemmed from perceived moments of helplessness. Fortunately, these emotions and reactions subsided as God provided me and my family with a place to both worship and heal from the wounds inflicted upon us by certain leaders and members of our previous church.

## ■ RELIGION

Job's reverence for God extends beyond personal desire, as reflected in his effort to secure his children's spiritual well-being. In the opening chapter of Job, we learn that "his sons used to hold feasts in their homes on their birthdays, and they would invite their three sisters to eat and drink with them. When a period of feasting had run its course, Job would make arrangements for them to be purified. Early in the morning, he would sacrifice a burnt offering for each of them, thinking, 'Perhaps my children have sinned and cursed God in their hearts.' This was Job's regular custom."[42] Francis Andersen writes of Job's spiritual sensitivity regarding his children:

> We need not suppose that they spent all their time in roistering and did no work. There is no hint of

---

[42] Job 1:4-5.

drunkenness or license or laziness. Job expresses no anxiety on this score, although he is aware of the danger that they might slip into profanity. These delightful family gatherings are part of the atmosphere of well-being that begins the story. They are a mark of good fortune, or rather of God's blessings. The finishing touch to this happy scene is the godly parent making doubly sure all is well.[43]

Job's spiritual sensitivity not only regarding his own life, but also the speech and conduct of his children serve as an example for pastors in being spiritually sensitive to the well-being of our churches, interceding on behalf of *all* congregants, which is not always easy. When on the receiving end of hostility from church leaders and members, pastors have a natural human tendency to gravitate toward those who are supportive and encouraging. Unfortunately, this also involves avoiding and withdrawing from others in the church who are engaging in and supporting the hostility. In extreme circumstances, this intentional and necessary disengagement from hostile members may also lead to omitting them from our prayers. Jesus provides us with biblical instructions on how to navigate these moments in the Sermon on the Mount when he says, "You have heard it was said, 'Love your neighbor and hate your enemy.' But I tell you, love your enemies and pray for those who persecute you, that you may be children of your Father in heaven. He causes his sun to rise on

---

[43] Francis I. Andersen, *Job: Tyndale OT Commentary Series* (London: InterVarsity Press, 1976), 80.

the evil and the good and sends rain on the righteous and the unrighteous. If you love those who love you, what reward will you get? Are not even the tax collectors doing that? And if you greet only your own people, what are you doing more than others? Do not even pagans do that? Be perfect, therefore, as your heavenly Father is perfect."[44]

It is clear by his statement that Jesus understands we will have enemies, even in the church. Like the relationship between Job and Satan, there may be some in the church who are intent on making life as difficult as possible for the pastor. Also, like Satan, their hatred and hostility intensify with time. The key is not allowing our enemies to have a negative impact on our responsibility to do everything for the glory of God. The hope is that loving your enemies will soften their hearts and cause them to reciprocate. The reality, however, is this does not always happen and pastors cannot stop loving those who continue engaging in hostile and sometimes hateful behavior.

## ■ MORALITY

Finally, we read that Job *shunned evil.* He committed his life to walking resolutely on the narrow road that leads to life, making every effort to avoid taking the broad road that leads so many to destruction. Job's authenticity was marked by continual repentance and a habitual turning away from evil in his actions, words, and even his thoughts. His morality is highlighted further in being declared

---

[44] Matt. 5:43–48.

by the Sovereign Lord as a man of righteousness along with Noah and Daniel.[45]

In *The Prayer of Jabez: Breaking through to the Blessed Life*, Bruce Wilkinson shares a helpful illustration about the necessity of turning away from evil:

> A full-page magazine ad depicts a Roman gladiator in big trouble. Somehow, he has dropped his sword. The enraged lion, seeing its opportunity, is in mid-lunge, jaws wide. The crowd in the Colosseum is on its feet, watching in horror as the panic-stricken gladiator tries to flee. The caption reads: Sometimes you can afford to come in second. Sometimes you can't. After asking for and receiving supernatural blessing, influence, and power, Jabez might have believed he could jump into any arena with any lion—and win. You would think that a person with the hand of God upon him would pray, "Keep me through evil." But Jabez understood what the doomed gladiator didn't: By far our most important strategy for defeating the roaring lion is to stay out of the arena. That's why the final request of his prayer was that God would keep him out of the fight: Oh ... keep me away from evil.[46]

---

[45] Ezek. 14:14, 20.

[46] Bruce Wilkinson, *The Prayer of Jabez: Breaking Through to the Blessed Life* (Sisters, OR: Multnomah Publishers, 2000), 62–63.

The ability of Jabez to sustain a blessed life stemmed from his petition for God to protect him from Satan's proven desire to see him fail and dishonor God.

Success in ministry certainly has its perks and rewards. But it also brings with it temptations and greater opportunities for failure. Consider some of the successful pastors who have fallen into sin and disappointed thousands of people along the way. These and other leaders who have fallen continue to teach us that the farther we climb in ministry, the more we will experience attacks that are designed to jeopardize our morality and ultimately destroy our reputations among people and our relationships with God.

When well-respected pastors fall into sin, the first question asked by many is why. To answer this commonly asked question, Crosswalk.com provided a list of "7 Surprising Reasons Christian Leaders Fall into Sin."[47] Prayerful consideration of its content will hopefully prevent others from engaging in immoral behaviors.

1. Say, "It Will Never Happen to Me"
   Pride makes Christian leaders believe that they would never lie, steal, or commit adultery. But it's precisely when we begin to think that we're not susceptible, that we fail to keep our guard up. We ignore conviction and the voice of the Holy Spirit.

---

[47] John Upchurch, "7 Surprising Reasons Christian Leaders Fall into Sin," *Crosswalk.com,* (June 2015), accessed August 28, 2019, https://www.crosswalk.com/blogs/christian-trends/7-surprising-reasons-christian-leaders-fall-into-sin.html.

2. Claim They're "Too Busy"

   According to Pastor Shane Idleman, "Nine times out of 10, when a leader falls, he or she has no meaningful prayer or devotional life." Business can become the excuse we use not to seek God and spend time with Him in prayer. But we cannot face the temptations of the world without this crucial practice. In other words, get on your knees more.

3. Compromise Holiness

   Failing leaders often think of holiness as another word for "legalism." But holiness is the very defense we need against the attack of our enemy (Ephesians 6:14). Without striving to live a life of purity, we begin rationalizing our moral failures instead of seeing the need to repent. "Sadly, Hollywood, not the Holy Spirit, influences many. We cannot fill our mind with darkness all week and expect the light of Christ to shine in our lives."

4. Build Unhealthy Relationships with the Opposite Sex

   When Christian leaders fall into adultery, we often find out that they had slowly developed a relationship with someone of the opposite sex—usually through small compromises here and there. They failed to build in the accountability structure that could have prevented the failure.

5. Fail to Strengthen Weak Areas

   It's much easier for us to hide our weak areas or to act like they don't exist. But we all have temptations that are especially difficult for us, whether drugs, alcohol, anger, pornography, or others. Denying those weak areas, however, will only allow Satan a foothold into our lives. We must get help right where we need it.

6. Breach Accountability

   No accountability system is perfect. We humans have ways of getting around just about anything when we want. Sometimes embarrassment keeps leaders and Christians in general from asking for prayer when the temptation arises or for allowing others to ask hard questions.

7. Use Loneliness as an Excuse

   When leaders feel lonely, they often use that as a reason for bad choices. But we must choose a better path, as Idleman says: "Sin can be silenced in a thankful heart set on worshipping God. God has given us the privilege to serve Him, proclaim His truth, and help others. Don't allow frustration and negativity to lead you down the wrong path.

At what appears to have been the most spiritually, physically, and emotionally challenging and excruciatingly painful time of his life, Job does not become a new Job. Instead, he continues living as the authentic man God created him to be through the daily practice of authenticity. As a reminder, "Authenticity is a process. It's something that continues to evolve throughout our entire lives. We can't become 'authentic' in the same way we can earn a degree or accomplish a financial goal. Authenticity—like love, health, courage, awareness, patience, and more—is an ideal we aspire to and is something we must practice in the moment-by-moment, day-by-day experiences of life. Our ability to be real can and will deepen as we move through our journey of life if we're conscious of it. Becoming more of who we really are is a process that never ends."[48] For Job, this process of practicing authenticity began long before God granted Satan permission to bring upon him this extraordinary accumulation of disasters.

In lieu of engaging in behaviors contrary to his usual God-fearing character, Job instead brings into his season of turmoil the aforementioned character traits used to describe him in the first verse of his story—blameless (integrity), upright (treatment of others), feared God (religion), and shunned evil (morality). While literally living within the grip of absolute evil and while facing continual relational confrontation with his friends Eliphaz, Bildad, and Zophar, God's Job remains God's Job.

Relative to Job's experience, this project is not about searching for a new authentic self during seasons of adversity. It speaks to maintaining and displaying one's constant authentic nature while enduring hostility from church members and while transitioning from a church where such hostility exists—either by resignation or termination. Although the information contained in this project may assist those who have intentionally caused their own pastoral demise, it is intended primarily to benefit those pastors who, like Job, are already in the habit of serving in righteousness and with the utmost integrity when the hostility surfaces.

In the end, God blesses Job for his faithfulness, and the order in which he does it is significant. He first restores their relationship, then he blesses him. Christopher Ash explains, "Job proves he is a real believer because he bows down to God in a time of pain. It is not that God first blesses him and then Job says, 'You seem to be a good God after all: I will worship you.' He worships because God

---

[48] Robbins, *Be Yourself, Everyone Else is Already Taken*, 4.

is God, and then in the end he is blessed. And when he worships he has no proof or certainty that he will be blessed. He lives by faith, not by sight."[49] The lesson each pastor should take from this is that there is a blessing in the end. After enduring the hostility, resisting temptations, sleepless nights, frustration, and even after resignation or termination, God has a blessing for you in the end.

---

[49] Ash, Job: The Wisdom of the Cross, 432.

CHAPTER 3

# MAINTAINING PASTORAL AUTHENTICITY

To explore the condition of "Maintaining Pastoral Authenticity through Resignation and Termination," interviews were conducted with senior pastors who successfully navigated their respective transitions through resignation or termination. Due to the COVID-19 restrictions imposed during my research, all except one of the interviews were conducted virtually with each lasting approximately two hours. The same list of twenty questions and statements was used to guide each conversation with the intent of maintaining a particular focus by eliciting responses and information specific to the topic at hand. Relative follow-up questions were also utilized. Each interviewee was thoroughly informed of the purpose of this project and willingly acknowledged their participation by signing the interview consent form, which, among other things, afforded them the option of declining to answer any of the interview questions and to withdraw from participating in this project at any time. To maintain confidentiality and anonymity, only an unsigned copy of this form is included as an appendix. The specific areas addressed in the interview consent form were as follows:

> **Purpose:** To explore various pastoral transition experiences ultimately resulting in the development and implementation of workshops, courses, and/ or other publications that will assist pastors in understanding and maintaining their authenticity through resignation and termination.

> **Procedure & Time Requirement:** If you consent, you will be asked several questions in an interview at a date, time, and location that is convenient for you. With your permission, I will make an audio recording of the interview that will only be used to create accurate written documentation. The interview, including any necessary follow-up conversations or clarification, will take approximately 1–2 hours of your time.

> **Voluntary Participation:** Your participation in this project is completely voluntary. If you choose to participate, you may still decline answering any of the interview questions that you do not want to answer. You may also withdraw from the interview at any time.

> **Confidentiality/Anonymity:** Your name will be kept confidential in all the reporting and

documentation related to this study. I will be the only person present for the interview and the only person who listens to any audio recordings. I will also use pseudonyms for all participants and organizations.

**Risks:** There are no known risks associated with this interview.

**Benefits:** While there are no guaranteed benefits, it is possible that you will experience a sense of purpose and relief in knowing that sharing your answers to the interview questions may eventually benefit pastors with similar experiences.

**Sharing the Results:** I plan to construct a written account of what I learn from my interviews, reading, research, and other collected data. This information will be submitted to my WTS Faculty Reader and the Doctor of Ministry Committee at scheduled times throughout this process.

**Publication:** The final version of this project will be submitted to the WTS Library and posted publicly in the Theological Research Exchange Network (TREN), where all WTS Doctor of Ministry projects have been preserved since 2011. There is also the possibility that I will publish this project or include portions of it in published writings in the future. If so, I will continue to use pseudonyms and may alter some personal and professional details to further protect your anonymity.

**Consent:** By signing below, you are agreeing to an interview for this project. Be sure that any questions you may have related to my project are answered to your satisfaction prior to signing. If you agree to participate in this project, you will be provided with a copy of this consent document.

## ■ THE INTERVIEWEES

The ministerial experience of the interviewees ranged from eight years to over thirty years with each having served anywhere between three and eight years as the senior pastor of the churches where they experienced the hostility that led to their resignation or termination. Each pastor also had a family to care for and provide for during their experiences and subsequent transition from their churches. Some were bivocational while others served in a full-time capacity. All the interviewees expressed their sincere appreciation for being invited to participate in this project, and most were willing to share very candidly about their individual experiences. While explaining the practice of confidentiality and anonymity related to this project, some of the interviewees expressed their approval for me to identify them and their churches by name. However, doing so could lead to the disclosure of the identities of those who wished to remain anonymous. Therefore, pseudonyms are used where necessary.

Each of the interviewees was serving as the senior pastor of a predominantly African American Baptist church. Knowing that pastors of other races, denominations, and cultures have endured hostile experiences that led to their resignation or termination, the decision was made to focus on the church context in which my personal experience also occurred. Sensing advises, "Your research cannot cover every conceivable angle or investigate every single interesting or pertinent idea. It must be keenly focused. Delimitations arbitrarily narrow the scope of your project. You delimit the project when you focus only on selected aspects, certain areas of interest, a restricted range of subjects, and a level of sophistication. Define your scope by setting boundaries."[50] These boundaries were established to produce a higher quality of research and reporting. They were also established to prevent the pursuit of potentially endless areas of interest. While interesting points surfaced during the interviews, addressing some of them would have moved this project outside of its intended scope.

## ■ REFLEXIVITY

According to Sensing,

> During the research process, investigators will also possess emotions. Recognizing how one's emotions affect the research process is known as *reflexivity*. Reflexivity is defined by Swinson and Mowat as "the process of critical self-reflection carried out by the researcher throughout the research process that enables her to monitor and

---

[50] Tim Sensing, *Qualitative Research: A Multi-Methods Approach to Projects for Doctor of Ministry Theses* (Eugene, OR: Wipf & Stock, 2011), 20.

respond to her contributions to the proceedings." Patton describes reflexivity under the category of voice and perspective. He states, The qualitative analysis owns and is reflective about her or his own voice and perspective; a credible voice conveys authenticity and trustworthiness; complete objectivity being impossible and pure subjectivity undermining credibility, the researcher's focus becomes balance—understanding and depicting the world authentically in all its complexity while being self-analytical, politically aware, and reflexive in consciousness.[51]

One of my biggest challenges during the development of this project was keeping my emotions in check. My personal experience with congregational hostility that led to my resignation was wrought with emotion, some of which still surfaces years later when I speak of specific aspects of that ordeal. To maintain the recommended balance necessary for completing this project, and being aware of my influence on it, I consciously reminded myself to "examine your emotional reactions to the setting, the study, and the participants"[52] during each interview to prevent my feelings from unknowingly or inappropriately shaping the interview/research process.

---

[51] Sensing, *Qualitative Research*, 43.

[52] Sherryl Kleinman, "Field Workers' Feelings: What We Feel, Who We Are, How We Analyze," in *Experiencing Fieldwork: An Inside View of Qualitative Research*, ed. William B. Shaffir and Robert A. Stebbins (Newbury Park, CA: Sage, 1991), 184.

# ▓ THE INTERVIEWS

During the course of the interviews and several preliminary conversations to clarify the purpose and scope of this project with the interviewees, commonalities related to how each pastor was able to maintain their authenticity were revealed in the following areas:

- Influence of the deacon board
- External pastoral influences
- "Church hurt"

## INFLUENCE OF THE DEACON BOARD

According to T. DeWitt Smith Jr.,

> One of the strongest misconceptions about the job of the deacon is the amount of influence and power that he considers he has. The contention and strife that grow from such erroneous thinking have their roots in the fact that the deacon of yesteryear was often the boss of the church. He gave the orders; his board was the "powers that be." If one wanted anything, including a pastor, he had to get the preapproval and permission of the deacon body. The chief problem that resulted in the black church was that the deacon brother saw himself as the church's overlord and not that of a spiritual undershepherd. It is a serious indictment against the churches of years past that they put powerful men in office to

serve as deacons instead of men with Spirit-power who saw it as their distinct privilege to serve the church. The problem has extended itself to these modern times in which we live.[53]

By far, this continuing problem with the influence and perceived authority of what is known as the deacon board in the African American Baptist church served as the biggest hindrance to the interviewees' ability to fully function in their pastoral calling and was a motivating factor in their leaving. Specific deacons were identified as leaders and instigators of the actions and events leading to their departure. Instead of working *with* the pastor by adopting the biblical model of mutual submission, they inappropriately acted as if they were called to be in charge of every aspect of the church, including the pastor. While there were deacons on the board who honored God and prayerfully supported their respective pastors while successfully serving the church body, they also unfortunately found themselves in the minority within a group that had come to view themselves as the governing authority of the church and wielded an influence that conflicted with the biblical purpose and characteristics associated with the office of the deacon.

The Bible identifies two offices of church leadership—pastors and deacons. It is the responsibility of the pastor to serve the church by providing spiritual leadership primarily through preaching, teaching, and administrative oversight. It is the responsibility of the deacons—godly men with servant's hearts—to serve by assisting with providing for the needs and care of families and individuals in

---

[53] T. DeWitt Smith, *The Deacon in the Black Baptist Church* (Pasadena: Hope Publishing House, 1993) 11.

the church and community. Using the sixth chapter of Acts, Paul Chappell provides us with a description of the characteristics of those initially chosen to serve in this role:[54]

*They had a godly influence.* The apostles instructed the church to "look ye among you." The men chosen had already exerted a godly influence that was noticed in the church—before they were given a position of church leadership.

*They had godly relationships.* The words "among you" note their ability to relate and get along with others. In addition to a right vertical relationship with the Lord, they had proper horizontal relationships with their church family.

*They had a godly reputation.* These were men of "honest report." They were men of integrity and honor, men whom the church could trust.

*They were full of wisdom.* These were not spiritual "wannabees." They were men who walked with God, yielded to the Holy Spirit, and were full of godly wisdom.

*They had a servant's heart.* The initial job given to these men was to serve the church widows. This was

---

[54] Paul Chappell, *The Ministry of the Baptist Deacon: A Handbook for Local Church Servant Leaders* (Lancaster, CA: Striving Together, 2010), 14.

not a glamorous job description, yet these men were chosen because of their willingness to serve.

*They were men of faith.* Because the pastor is the overseer of the church, the men who serve with him must have faith to follow their pastor.

Most of the interviewees expressed their appreciation for those who served faithfully and supportively during their transitions while exhibiting these biblical characteristics. The deacons they identified were a blessing to their churches and pastors, as both were impacted by each unfortunate experience and outcome. They also understood how important the pastor-deacon relationship was to the health of the church body. For some of the interviewees, there were specific deacons with whom they had become friends and from whom they had received continual prayer and occasional counsel. A key characteristic mentioned in describing these deacons was their being motivated not by a self-serving agenda, but by the Holy Spirit and a desire to glorify God in their service: "This is the kind of leader that God entrusts with influence, and it is the kind of leader that God's people can follow with willing-hearted sincerity."[55]

## EXTERNAL PASTORAL INFLUENCE

A somewhat surprising factor involved in the experience of some of the pastors interviewed was the opposing negative influences of fellow pastors serving within their respective local communities. For reasons known and unknown, leading clergy outside of the churches

---

[55] Chappell, *The Ministry of a Baptist Deacon*, 31.

being addressed in this project provided support and guidance to internal factions focused on removing their respective pastors by resignation or termination. One interviewee described the actions of these pastors as cowardly, as many of them operated in secrecy. Complicating things further for certain interviewees were the long-lasting relationships between these intruding pastors and members of the interviewees' churches, relationships that were founded on years of biblically misleading practices designed to build a sense of congregational trust in the pastoral leadership of the outsiders. Additionally, there were local pastors who intentionally influenced their own congregations as well as other clergies by sharing false information related to the conflict between the interviewee and their congregation.

While the negative influence of external pastors impacted the interviewees, there were other pastors whose involvement was very much appreciated. These relationships will be mentioned later in this chapter. The interviewees who experienced this negative pastoral influence expressed their desire for this important aspect of their transitions to be highlighted in this project so that others in similar situations are aware of its potential presence.

## "CHURCH HURT"

Considering the blatant hostility experienced during my transition, I intentionally invited pastors who endured similar forms and degrees of hostility to participate in this project. Related conversations during the interview process often led to the use of the term "church hurt," which is commonly used to describe the intentional and unintentional pain inflicted upon believers by church leaders, church members, and church practices. Frank Thomas rightfully states, "Church hurt is the worst of all hurts. Why? Because the church is the place where you expect to get help and healing for all the other hurts of life. The church is the place where you bring the divorce hurt, the layoff hurt, the affair hurt, and the bankruptcy hurt. When you are hurt in church, you run the risk of having no place to bring your hurt, save directly to God."[56]

Church hurt is significant because it stems from the people and places where the hurt is expected to be relieved, not intensified. The victims of church hurt often leave the offending church and avoid immediately joining another, possibly feeling as if there is no physical place to express and deposit their personal pain. I have even had victims of church hurt tell me that the hurt they experienced was caused by having details of their revealed personal hurt used as weapons against them. Divorce, finances, and immoral behavior of the victims and their immediate family members are some of the more common weapons I have been made aware of.

Church hurt is also very real for pastors, as many have experienced it stemming mostly from the aforementioned deacon board. The office of the deacon, or diaconate, as explained by Alexander Strauch, "is not a ruling or governing office. The word *overseer* itself and the qualifications and duties prescribed of the overseer-elders demonstrate that overseers protect, teach, and lead the church. The term *diakonos* indicates an office of service, not of rule."[57] However, as the interviewees expressed and other pastors

---

[56] Frank A. Thomas, *The Choice: Living Your Passion Inside Out* (Indianapolis: Hope For Life International Books, 2013), 115–116.

[57] Alexander Strauch, *The New Testament Deacon: Minister of Mercy*, (Littleton, CO: Lewis & Roth, 1992), 74.

know, many deacons often misunderstand their biblical role and sometimes function as if their work is independent of the leadership oversight of the pastor. Each of the interviewees was fully aware of this common flaw in the leadership structure of their respective churches prior to accepting their pastoral posts. The consensus, unfortunately, is that this is a problem in the church that most pastors anticipate as they prepare for the inevitable conflict resulting from this spiritual and organizational defect.

## ■ MAINTAINING PASTORAL AUTHENTICITY

As highlighted by this project, the conflict between pastors and deacons, and the added congregational hostility it promotes, can sometimes only be overcome with the resignation or termination of the pastor. Very rarely, if ever, will a church remove deacons from office during such conflict. This experience takes a definite toll on the pastors involved, especially in the cases where the deacons involved took actions that intentionally publicized what should have remained an internal dilemma. Similar to my experience of being prevented access to my office during my transition, the interviewees shared stories that included not being permitted to enter the church building on Sunday morning to preach and lead worship services and the defacing of external church signage to indicate the pastor had been removed prior to the church having officially made any such determination.

The shared challenge for the participating pastors was remaining true to who God made and called them to be while navigating their respective storms. In addition to dealing with the continual conflict, each had to deal with the accompanying mental and emotional impact of personal grief and professional loneliness. To handle the admittedly hurtful emotional experiences, the interviewees employed practices and behaviors consistent with the following suggested strategies from H. B. London that are helpful in dealing with the pain caused by leaving a church.[58] These are also strategies the participating pastors would advise others to practice during their transition and following their departure.

***Use your grief skills.*** *As an experienced pastor, think back on ways you helped people deal with loss in their lives. Remember how grief washes over one like waves—in the midst of the apparent calm, a great breaker appears from nowhere.*

Tapping into pastoral practices used in leading others through grief and loneliness proved beneficial in overcoming the mental and emotional impact of such a transitional experience. One pastor even mentioned having experienced the five stages of grief during his transition—*denial, anger, bargaining, depression,* and *acceptance*—all while continuing to preach and pastor those who were willing to follow and accept his leadership.

While there are a number of strategies employed by pastors in counseling others experiencing grief, the area consistently mentioned or implied was that which dealt with the concept of perseverance. Each of the pastors undoubtedly recognized that the successful outcome of their internal and external battles depended on their ability to persevere in faith by continuing steadfastly in their relationships with Jesus Christ. Keeping this relationship at the forefront of their engagement with church hostility provided

---

[58] H. B. London and Neil Wiseman, *They Call Me Pastor: How to Love the Ones You Lead* (Ventura: Regal Books, 2000), 59–61.

the daily assurance and encouragement needed. Jay Adams writes, "Counselors must say in no uncertain terms that if they are truly saints (God's own), it *does* matter; *He* cares. And saints *will* persevere; sooner or later they will come to realize this, so they might as well face it now and get out of their doldrums, self-pity (or whatever) and begin to act like saints."[59] Along these lines, although none of the interviewees had reached the point of doldrums or self-pity, there was comfort in being constantly reminded that God cares and their perseverance—as saints—was a certainty.

***Tell God your feelings.*** *Tell the Father in your prayers how confused you are about leaving and starting again. Ask Him why you feel such a sense of loss when you are sure He has directed you to your new assignment. The dialogue will strengthen you.*

Although spiritual fitness is a quality found in those called to provide pastoral leadership, it is also possible for pastors to become spiritually out of shape. This normally has nothing to do with conflict or hostility. It is a condition that gradually surfaces as one performs the seemingly endless duties associated with pastoring often with a relatively unstructured schedule. Not to mention those who are bivocational and have the added responsibility of devoting a large window of their time to another employer, leaving them to fulfill their pastoral duties often during late evenings and weekends. Whether one is bivocational or serving in full-time ministry, it is easy for a pastor to unknowingly allow church busyness to take away from their spiritual self-care and lead to frustration, anger, weariness, and other spiritually and physically unhealthy feelings.

---

[59] Jay Adams, *A Theology of Christian Counseling: More than Redemption* (Grand Rapids: Zondervan, 1979), 270.

And this occurs during relatively normal times in the life of the church.

These conditions and feelings are significantly compounded when a pastor is experiencing the added chaos of being forced to choose between resignation or potential termination. In these times when it seems as if everything is working against us, when all of our efforts at peacemaking have failed, it is extremely imperative for pastors to be intentional about sharing their feelings with God in prayer. "We're not sure we can face another day, and yet we see an unending number of days of difficulty ahead. In these moments, when we realize all of our human resources have failed, we are most open to requesting the power of God."[60] It is in God's power that each of the interviewees was able to persevere and grow closer to Him in the throes of personal and professional conflict.

***Listen to spiritually mature friends and advisors.*** *Those who have lived for a few years have a lot to teach us if we are ready to learn.*

There was a consistent acknowledgment of how helpful it was to have at least one trusted friend or mentor to whom the interviewees could confide and to whom they could make themselves accountable. In addition to being able to pour out their feelings before them, these were people who also had been given permission to "pry" into areas of the pastor's life to where very few people had been given access. Most importantly, this confidant must love the hurting pastor enough to "listen redemptively to his hurts, to affirm his strengths and to call

---

[60] Dan Schaeffer, *The Power of Weakness: Embracing the True Source of Strength* (Grand Rapids: Discovery House, 2014), 88.

him to authenticity. He must know when to pat the pastor on the back and when to kick him in the seat."[61]

Aware of the number of people continually praying for them through each ordeal, the participants acknowledged that only another pastor could relate and be most helpful. Even if they had not gone through this exact experience, a seasoned pastor would likely connect and be equipped to offer an authentic blend of guidance and support. One of the participants admitted to being surprised by the advice he received from an older, vastly experienced pastor. Expecting to be encouraged to "hang in there" and "weather the storm," he instead was told in no uncertain terms that it was time for him to leave the church. What the older pastor followed with, however, is what provided the participating pastor with some desperately needed clarity and focus during his transition. The wiser pastor explained that leaving the church did not excuse him from fulfilling his pastoral duties to those God placed in his care until his final day in office and that he would be holding him accountable for this throughout the transitional process. This wise counsel from a trusted friend and advisor not only helped the pastor in his departure but also provided him with an opportunity to strengthen his relationship with God in ways he admitted he likely would have avoided if not for this enlightening guidance and accountability.

As previously mentioned, the negative influence of outside pastors was a contributing factor in the conflict experienced by some of the interviewees. Having a mature believer with whom to discuss this aspect of the encounter assisted in avoiding the mistake

---

[61] H.B. London and Neil Wiseman, *The Heart of a Great Pastor: How to Grow Strong and Thrive Wherever God Has Planted You* (Ventura: Regal Books, 1994), 187.

of giving these unwelcomed pastors a place of priority on the list of problems needing to be addressed. Doing so would have likely created a secondary battle that would have drained the interviewees of the energy and focus needed to persevere while honoring God.

**Use your grief to make you a better pastor.** *Thomas Jefferson's insightful quote teaches us how grief can help us: "Grief drives men to the habits of serious reflection, sharpens the understanding and softens the heart."*

All except one of the interviewees continued serving in pastoral ministry and were blessed to inherit or establish new congregations. The interviewee who is no longer pastoring a church successfully used their departure as an opportunity to pursue their passion to serve in a somewhat related profession and was doing extremely well at the time of the interview. Each has found success beyond the conflict with their former churches by using what could have been a destructive experience to enhance their pastoral and leadership skills while also growing increasingly closer to God.

Interestingly, one of the avenues to becoming a better pastor was found in continuing to lovingly preach and teach the gospel during a time when that love was not always reciprocated. During storms of disagreement and conflict, there is a real temptation for the pastor to engage in revenge preaching that is addressed by H. Beecher Hicks:

> I know from personal experience that the storm definitely affects the preaching engagement. Many advised me in the midst of the storm to go to the pulpit and "simply preach Jesus!" Others encouraged me to keep the message upbeat and positive. Easier said than done, my friend! It is no simple matter for

a preacher caught in the throes of a storm to remain objective and fair. The storm provides an unnatural, alien, even hostile environment in which preaching with power becomes nearly impossible. There are rare moments when the reverse is true—when the conflict provides grist for the mill, so to speak, and the challenge brings out the best in the preacher. More often than not, however, the preacher is prone to want to "fight back," to make a pulpit response to the forces working against him. In doing so he loses both a measure of his integrity as a preacher and the preaching perspective required of a pastor ... The preacher must always be willing to examine his motivation and remain sensitive to the psychological power of the sermon. And he should seek to be positive. But he must never flinch from declaring revealed truth either. Clearly, however, to will and to do are vastly different things.[62]

The urge to fight back mentioned by Hicks most likely reveals itself initially in sermon preparation, which gives the preacher ample time to resist it and carefully structure a God-honoring message rather than one that confronts the critics and gives the preacher a "lopsided advantage that too often results in a biased presentation of my side of the story without an opportunity for a fair rebuttal."[63]

---

[62] H. Beecher Hicks, *Preaching Through a Storm: Confirming the Power of Preaching in the Tempest of Church Conflict* (Grand Rapids: Zondervan, 1987), 16–17.

[63] Preston, *Pastors in Pain*, 65.

Unfortunately, this ideal outcome is not always reached. Those who have been more successful than others at resisting the temptation to write and preach revenge sermons acknowledged having trusted voices like those previously mentioned to guide them in this area of ministry. The preacher was able to unload their frustrations and other emotions during the week and relieve themselves of the need to do so on Sunday mornings.

# CHAPTER 4

# CREATING AN EMPTY SPACE

The initial purpose of this project was to fill a perceived void of information specifically addressing the ability of pastors to maintain their authenticity when facing resignation and termination. Interviewing several pastors who had left a pastoral position by choice or by force while experiencing congregational hostility was a key component to gaining a better understanding of an unfortunate dynamic that occurs far too often. During the interview process, this project became more than a fact-finding tool. It also developed into a place of healing through the sharing of painful experiences. In conversation, the researcher and participants began living out the words of Henri J. M. Nouwen: "A shared pain is no longer paralyzing but mobilizing when understood as a way to liberation."[64] While many had previously shared stories of their experiences with

---

[64] Henri Nouwen, *The Wounded Healer: In Our Own Woundedness, We Can Become a Source of Life for Others* (New York: Doubleday, 1979), 93.

others, none had done so in a setting such as this that provided a platform to further the healing that had begun years ago.

Whether acknowledged or not, there was a sense of loneliness felt by all that was exceedingly more intense than the loneliness that is an integral part of the pastorate. It is the feeling of loneliness that is especially painful when it stems from the hostile behaviors of the very people to whom the pastor directs an outpouring of love. A natural response to this loneliness is for one to search for freedom from isolation through fellowship with others or by engaging in an overabundance of activities—both constructive and destructive—as an escape from this undesired reality. On the contrary, this project became an avenue through which each of us could discuss our experienced loneliness as "an inexhaustible source of beauty and self-understanding."[65]

Nouwen uses the word *hospitality* to describe the way of healing for the Christian minister, stating that "hospitality asks for the creation of an empty space where the guest can find his own soul."[66] For many, this project developed into that empty space where we engaged in a significant amount of soul-searching en route to even more peace and spiritual growth in addition to that which occurred since leaving the churches and congregations in question. Instead of avoiding the pain, frustration, and loneliness associated with leaving a church under harsh conditions, these emotions were recognized and shared as a means of continued personal healing and in an effort to help other pastors who may need to hear that their wounds can also become a source of healing.

---

[65] Nouwen, *The Wounded Healer*, 84.

[66] Ibid., 92.

## ■ RECOMMENDATIONS

The following recommendations are provided to assist anyone who is considering conducting a similar project. Items that were part of this project such as the interview consent form and the interview questions are included as appendices.

*Take the necessary time to thoroughly prescreen interviewees.* Being focused solely on identifying interviewees that have been forced to resign from a church or were unfairly terminated, I lost sight of the possibility that some who lived through this type of experience may not have been willing to share their story in a way that productively assisted in completing this project. I found that there was a very small percentage who wanted to share their stories but were not willing to do so in a way that benefited this project. A lesson was learned as valuable hours were lost listening as those who mistakenly understood my purpose proceeded to seemingly brag about their courageous accomplishments during their transitions while simultaneously offering me poor advice on how I could have better handled my own experience by responding as they had to theirs.

In these instances, it is recommended that the interviewer immediately discontinue the interview when it becomes clear it is not accomplishing its intended purpose. I assumed providing the interviewee with directions would lead to a more productive conversation only to find myself listening as my instructions were ignored. According to Sensing, "The main purpose of the interview is to obtain a special kind of information."[67] An interview that is not leading to obtaining the desired information should be discontinued.

---

[67] Sensing, *Qualitative Research*, 104.

*Be aware of your own subdued emotions related to your project.* In chapter 3, I addressed the topic of reflexivity which involves continual self-reflection with the intent of preventing the emotions of the interviewer from unknowingly or inappropriately shaping the interview/research process. The interviews, especially those where the interviewee is a friend or close acquaintance, may provide opportunities to inappropriately sway the direction of the process and negatively influence the way in which the interviewer addresses the interview questions and provides other pertinent feedback. This awareness, coupled with continued self-reflection, will undoubtedly assist in providing the balance needed to maintain the integrity of the project.

This project allowed the researcher and participating pastors to explore how each of us was able to grow considerably in our relationships with God through what some described as one of the most difficult pastoral experiences imaginable. Sincere self-examination in a trusted setting led to the reviving of old emotions as well as to the revelation of new ones. As spiritually enlightening as this process was for all involved, the consensus is that the information provided will help others to maintain their pastoral authenticity through resignation and termination.

As mentioned in the introduction, the ultimate goal of this project is to encourage pastors to remain true to who God not only *called* them to be, but also to be true to who God *created* them to be, especially when facing congregational conflict and hostility. Prayerfully, this project will serve as a reminder to remain grounded in the fundamental values with which most of us accepted the call of God to lead others to lifelong faith in Jesus Christ.

# INTERVIEW CONSENT FORM

My name is Michael Palmer, and I am in the dissertation phase of my doctoral studies at Wesley Theological Seminary (WTS). I am requesting your participation in my final project which is outlined in this consent form. If you have any questions about this project, please contact me at (###) ###-####.

**Title:** Maintaining Pastoral Authenticity through Resignation and Termination

**Purpose:** To explore various pastoral transition experiences ultimately resulting in the development and implementation of workshops, courses, and/or other publications that will assist pastors in understanding and maintaining their authenticity through resignation and termination.

**Procedure & Time Requirement:** If you consent, you will be asked several questions in an interview at a date, time, and location that is convenient for you. With your permission, I will make an audio recording of the interview that will only be used to create accurate written documentation. The interview, including any necessary follow-up conversations or clarification, will take approximately 1–2 hours of your time.

**Voluntary Participation:** Your participation in this project is completely voluntary. If you choose to participate, you may still decline to answer any of the interview questions that you do not want to answer. You may also withdraw from the interview at any time.

**Confidentiality/Anonymity:** Your name will be kept confidential in all the reporting and documentation related to this study. I will be the only person present for the interview and the only person who listens to any audio recordings. I will also use pseudonyms for all participants and organizations.

**Risks:** There are no known risks associated with this interview.

**Benefits:** While there are no guaranteed benefits, it is possible that you will experience a sense of purpose and relief in knowing that sharing your answers to the interview questions may eventually benefit pastors with similar experiences.

**Sharing the Results:** I plan to construct a written account of what I learn from my interviews, reading, research, and other collected data. This information will be submitted to my WTS Faculty

Reader and the Doctor of Ministry Committee at scheduled times throughout this process.

**Publication:** The final version of this project will be submitted to the WTS Library and posted publicly in the Theological Research Exchange Network (TREN), where all WTS Doctor of Ministry projects have been preserved since 2011. There is also the possibility that I will publish this project or include portions of it in published writings in the future. If so, I will continue to use pseudonyms and may alter some personal and professional details to further protect your anonymity.

**Consent:** By signing below, you are agreeing to an interview for this project. Be sure that any questions you may have related to my project are answered to your satisfaction prior to signing. If you agree to participate in this project, you will be provided with a copy of this consent document.

Thank you for your consideration.

Participant: _____ Signature: _____ Date_____

Researcher: _____ Signature: _____ Date_____

# INTERVIEW QUESTIONS

Thank you for participating in this project as an interviewee. Below is a list of questions and statements that may be used to guide our interview/conversation. Follow-up/additional questions may be included. As stated in the Interview Consent Form, you may decline to answer any of the interview questions that you do not want to answer or discuss any particular topic. You may also withdraw from this project at any time.

1. Tell me about your pastoral experience and how you came to be the pastor of the church in question (years pastoring, number and types of churches, seminary or other relative schooling/education, family, etc.).

2. What attracted you to this particular church? What motivated you to pursue the pastorate there?

3. Tell me about the interview process. Did you notice any red flags?

4. Describe the church at which you experienced termination or resignation (denomination, size, culture, etc.).

5. How long were you the pastor of this church?

6. How would you define "pastoral authenticity"?

7. How did your pastoral authenticity factor into the difficulties experienced in leading this church?

8. What role did your pastoral authenticity play in your resignation or termination?

9. What specific event or series of events led to your leaving this church? What were the specific difficulties?

10. Who were the key players (i.e., elders, deacons, trustees, etc.) who influenced your resignation or termination?

11. What were some of the behaviors/tactics/tricks used by those who intentionally made it difficult for you to remain at this church?

12. How difficult was your transition (emotionally, financially, etc.)? How well did you handle it?

13. Did you consider or receive counseling to help you deal with your termination or resignation?

14. Was there a severance offered/available upon your termination or resignation?

15. Did you have other employment or means of income upon your termination or resignation?

16. How did fear factor into your termination or resignation?

17. How were your relationships with other pastors affected by your termination or resignation?

18. How was your spouse/family affected by this experience?

19. What lessons did you take away from this experience?

20. What advice would you offer pastors dealing with experiences similar to yours?

# BIBLIOGRAPHY

Adams, Jay. *A Theology of Christian Counseling: More than Redemption*. Grand Rapids: Zondervan, 1979.

Andersen, Francis. *Job: Tyndale OT Commentary Series*. London: InterVarsity Press, 1976.

Ash, Christopher. *Job: The Wisdom of the Cross*. Wheaton, IL: Crossway, 2014.

Bohm, David. *On Dialogue*. London: Routledge, 1996.

Brown, Brené. *The Gifts of Imperfection: Let Go of Who You Think You're Supposed to Be and Embrace Who You Are*. Center City, MN: Hazelden, 2010.

Chappell, Paul. *The Ministry of a Baptist Deacon: Handbook for Local Church Servant Leaders*. Lancaster, CA: Striving Together, 2010.

Clemance, C. "The Epistles of St. John." In *The Pulpit Commentary, Volume 22: Epistles of Peter, John & Jude. The Revelation*.

Edited by H.D.M. Spence and Joseph Exell. Peabody, MA: Hendrickson, 1985.

Dale, Robert. *Pastoral Leadership*. Nashville: Abingdon Press, 1986.

Hicks, H. Beecher. *Preaching Through a Storm: Confirming the Power of Preaching in the Tempest of Church Conflict*. Grand Rapids: Zondervan, 1987.

Kleinman, Sherryl. "Field Workers' Feelings: What We Feel, Who We Are, How We Analyze." In *Experiencing Fieldwork: An Inside View of Qualitative Research*. Edited by William Shaffir and Robert Stebbins. Newbury Park, CA: Sage, 1991.

Lickerman, Alex. "The Value of a Good Reputation: Why We Should Care About How Others Perceive Us." *Psychology Today* (April 2010). Accessed October 3, 2019. https://www.psychologytoday.com/us/blog/happiness-in-world/201004/the-value-good-reputation.

London, H.B. and Neil Wiseman. *The Heart of a Great Pastor: How to Grow Strong and Thrive Wherever God Has Planted You*. Ventura: Regal Books, 1994.

———. *They Call Me Pastor: How to Love the Ones You Lead*. Ventura: Regal Books, 2000.

Maxwell, John, and Jim Dornan. *Becoming a Person of Influence: How to Positively Impact the Lives of Others*. Nashville: Thomas Nelson, 1997.

McCormick, Blaine, and David Davenport. *Shepherd Leadership: Wisdom for Leaders from Psalm 23*. San Francisco: Jossey-Bass, 2003.

Nouwen, Henri. *The Wounded Healer: In Our Own Woundedness, We Can Become a Source of Life for Others*. New York: Doubleday, 1979.

Osborne, Larry. *Lead Like a Shepherd: The Secret to Leading Well*. Nashville: Thomas Nelson, 2018.

Peters, Tim. "10 Reasons Why Pastors Quit Too Soon." *Church Leaders* (April 2016). Accessed September 16, 2019. https://churchleaders.com/pastors/pastor-articles/161343-tim_peters_10_common_reasons_pastors_quit_too_soon.html.

Petersen, Eugene. "Introduction to Job." In *The Message*. Colorado Springs: NavPress, 2002.

Preston, Gary. *Pastors in Pain: How to Grow in Times of Conflict*. Grand Rapids: Baker Books, 1999.

Rainer, Thom. *Autopsy of a Deceased Church: 12 Ways to Keep Yours Alive*. Nashville: B&H, 2014.

Rawlinson, G. "Job." In *The Pulpit Commentary, Volume 7: Ezra, Nehemiah, Esther & Job*. Edited by H.D.M. Spence and Joseph Exell. Peabody, MA: Hendrickson, 1985.

Rendle, Gil. "Narrative Leadership and Renewed Congregational Identity." In *Finding Our Story: Narrative Leadership and*

*Congregational Change*. Edited by Larry Golemon. Lanham, MD: Rowman & Littlefield, 2010.

Robbins, Mike. *Be Yourself: Everyone Else is Already Taken*. San Francisco: Jossey- Bass, 2009.

Schaeffer, Dan. *The Power of Weakness: Embracing the True Source of Strength*. Grand Rapids: Discovery House, 2014.

Sensing, Tim. *Qualitative Research: A Multi-Methods Approach to Projects for Doctor of Ministry Theses*. Eugene: Wipf & Stock, 2011.

Smith, T. DeWitt. *The Deacon in the Black Church*. Pasadena: Hope Publishing House, 1993.

Strauch, Alexander. *The New Testament Deacon: Minister of Mercy*. Littleton, CO: Lewis & Roth, 1992.

Thomas, Frank. *The Choice: Living Your Passion Inside Out*. Indianapolis: Hope for Life International Books, 2013.

Upchurch, John. "7 Surprising Reasons Christian Leaders Fall into Sin." *Crosswalk.com* (June 2015). Accessed August 28, 2019. https://www.crosswalk.com/blogs/christian-trends/7-surprising-reasons-christian-leaders-fall-into-sin.html.

Webb, Henry. *Deacons: Servant Models in the Church*. Nashville: B&H, 2001.

Wilkinson, Bruce. *The Prayer of Jabez: Breaking Through to the Blessed Life*. Sisters, OR: Multnomah Publishers, 2000.

Printed in the United States
by Baker & Taylor Publisher Services